Italian
Essentials

by Teresa L. Picarazzi, PhD

A Wiley Brand

Italian Essentials For Dummies®

Published by: **John Wiley & Sons, Inc.**, 111 River Street, Hoboken, NJ 07030-5774, www.wiley.com

The manufacturer's authorized representative according to the EU General Product Safety Regulation is Wiley-VCH GmbH, Boschstr. 12, 69469 Weinheim, Germany, email: Product_Safety@wiley.com.

For general information on our other products and services, please contact our Customer Care Department within the U.S. at 877-762-2974, outside the U.S. at 317-572-3993, or fax 317-572-4002. For technical support, please visit https://hub.wiley.com/community/support/dummies.

Wiley publishes in a variety of print and electronic formats and by print-on-demand. Some material included with standard print versions of this book may not be included in e-books or in print-on-demand. If this book refers to media that is not included in the version you purchased, you may download this material at http://booksupport.wiley.com. For more information about Wiley products, visit www.wiley.com.

Library of Congress Control Number is available from the publisher.

ISBN 978-1-394-37328-4 (pbk); ISBN 978-1-394-37329-1 (ebk); ISBN 978-1-394-37330-7 (ebk)

Printed and bound by CPI Group (UK) Ltd, Croydon, CR0 4YY

C9781394373284_041125

Table of Contents

Introduction

As someone who's studying Italian, you want to be proficient enough to write and speak correctly, which involves having a knowledgeable grasp of grammar and finding your way and being more comfortable with the many different verb tenses and conjugations. *Italian Essentials For Dummies* can help you set and reach your goals painlessly as you enhance your Italian language skills.

This handy guide presents you with the basics of grammar and vocabulary in context that you need to know to understand and be understood, in both written and spoken Italian. With the help of this book, you'll be ready to have a conversation about topics besides your name and where you are from! And that's something to be proud of.

About This Book

Italian Essentials For Dummies is a reference book for people who already have some knowledge of the fundamentals of Italian and want to refresh the essentials. If you want to get up to speed with language structures so that you can navigate the language comfortably and proficiently, this book is for you. Because I spell things out for you, it's also okay if you're an absolute beginner.

Each chapter presents a different topic that allows you to strengthen your grammar knowledge and accuracy. I offer an array of examples to guide you through the rules so you're exposed to colloquial, everyday, correct Italian that heritage speakers expect to hear from someone using Italian. For example, the Italian language has its individual idiomatic expressions that give it color and flair. Here's a quick example: To say that you're 40 years old in Italian, you remark, **Ho quaranta anni.** The literal English translation of this expression is *I have forty years.* That's good to know, because asking for and providing personal information is often a great ice-breaker and way to get to know someone.

In order to highlight the most important information and to help you navigate this book more easily, I use the following conventions:

>> Italian terms and sentences, as well as endings I want to highlight, are set in **boldface** to make them stand out.

>> English equivalents, set in *italics* and in parentheses, follow the Italian example.

>> I use many abbreviations throughout the book. Don't let them throw you. For instance, you may find the following:

- **fem.:** feminine
- **masc.:** masculine
- **sing.:** singular
- **pl.:** plural

Foolish Assumptions

When writing this book, I made the following assumptions:

>> You have some knowledge of the fundamentals of Italian grammar. You're looking for the opportunity to review what you've already mastered and are intent on moving forward to new areas of knowledge.

>> You want a book that's complete but isn't so advanced that you get lost in the rules. I try to explain the rules as clearly as possible without using too many grammatical terms.

>> You're honing your Italian for your own edification — maybe you're taking a trip to Italy soon — or your son, daughter, grandson, granddaughter, niece, nephew, or special someone is studying Italian and you want to help, even though you haven't thought about verb conjugations for years.

Icons Used in This Book

Icons are those cute little drawings on the left side of the page that call out for your attention. They signal a particularly valuable piece of information. Here's a list of the icons in this book:

REMEMBER

Remember icons call your attention to important information about the language — something you shouldn't neglect or something that's out of the ordinary. Don't ignore these paragraphs.

TIP

Tip icons present time-saving information that makes communication quick and effective. If you want to know the proper way to do things, check out the Tip icons first.

WARNING

The Warning icon points out certain differences between English and Italian that you may find confusing. If you want to know how Italian constructions differ from those in English, you need to read these paragraphs.

Where to Go from Here

One great thing about *For Dummies* books is that you don't have to read them chapter by chapter from the very beginning to the bitter end. Each chapter stands on its own and doesn't require that you complete any of the other chapters in the book. I provide you with plenty of cross-referencing if you need to jump ahead or behind for greater clarity. This setup saves you a lot of time if you've mastered certain topics but feel a bit insecure about others.

So, dive right in. Get your feet wet. If you're not sure exactly where to begin, look at the table of contents and select the topic that piques your abilities and needs. If you're concerned that your background may not be strong enough, you can start at the very beginning and work your way through the book.

Keep in mind that studying Italian isn't a contest. Work at a pace that best suits your needs. Don't hesitate to read a chapter a second or even third time several days later. You can easily adapt this book to your learning abilities.

Italian is a living language that requires listening, speaking, and writing practice. From the very beginning, challenge yourself to engage more directly with the language by referencing online sources that allow you to listen to and practice speaking the sounds of Italian. You can start with the alphabet and days of the week and work your way up to music and film. Locate a study buddy or find an Italian pen pal. You can also get direct writing practice with other Italian *For Dummies* publications (published by John Wiley & Sons, Inc.).

Making mistakes is okay. Everyone makes them — as a matter of fact, many Italian heritage speakers do all the time. Your main goal should be to communicate as well as you can, both orally and in written form. If you trip up and conjugate a verb incorrectly or use the feminine form of an adjective rather than the masculine form, it isn't the end of the world. As long as you can understand and make yourself understood, you've won the greatest part of the battle.

While using this book, keep in mind that Italian continues to change and to adapt insofar as vocabulary, pronunciation, and the use of language forms.

Furthermore, English influence on Italian continues to evolve, especially among younger speakers. English words and phrases referring to modern technology have been incorporated into Italian, such as the word *app*. For example, you can see several examples of this phenomenon by reading the lyrics and listening to the singer Fedez's **Vorrei ma non posto** (*I'd like to but I don't post*, which is a play on words of the very common phrase, **Vorrei, ma non posso,** *I'd like to, but I can't.*).

Gender inclusivity and recent usage have paved the way for new vocabulary that denotes professions. For example, you can now say **poeta** to refer to both a male and a female poet, whereas once upon a time there was the masculine **il poeta** and the feminine **la poetessa**. Same thing for **avvocato** for both genders (instead of **avvocatessa** for a woman).

The use of the formal plural **loro** (*you, pl.*) is disappearing in favor of the informal **voi** (*you pl.*).

Now you're all set and ready to begin perfecting your Italian language skills. **Uno, due, tre, via!** (*One, two, three, go!*) **In bocca al lupo!** (*Good luck!*).

IN THIS CHAPTER

» Perfecting your pronunciation

» Getting to know you

» Counting and putting two and two together

» Exploring dates

» Telling time versus asking at what time?

» Brushing up on the basics with parts of speech

Chapter **1**

Focusing on the Basics

Y ou're reading this book because you're interested in learn-ing Italian or brushing up on what you already know — **molto bene!** *(great!)* You're in the right place: **Benvenute/ Benvenuti!** *(Welcome!)*

What are some essential first steps in getting your feet wet in another language? This chapter introduces you to important Italian skills that aid in everyday spoken and written communica-tion as it walks you through pronunciation, greetings, numbers, time, basic parts of speech, and gender. Although you need to approach the language holistically and in context, you also have to grasp the individual parts of the whole, which is where this book comes in.

REMEMBER

Italian is a living language. I can't emphasize enough how impor-tant it is for you to practice saying and hearing Italian while you go through this book. I highly recommend finding sources online, from the alphabet to podcasts, to music, to television series. I also suggest you consult the latest edition of *Italian For Dummies* by Giuseppe Cavatorta and me, and my *Italian Workbook for Dummies* (John Wiley & Sons, Inc.), for more on Italian pronunciation and direct application of skills and practice dialogues.

Mouthing Off: Basic Pronunciation

Italian provides many opportunities for your tongue to do acrobatics. This is really fun, because the language offers you some new sounds. In this section, I give you some basic pronunciation hints that are important both for surfing through this book and for good articulation when you speak Italian. If you learn the correct pronunciation in this chapter, starting with the alphabet, you'll be reading and speaking like a real Italian in no time.

These sections provide you with a rough phonetic spelling of the Italian pronunciation, just to get you started. Place extra *umph* on the stressed (*italicized*) syllables.

The alphabet

What better way is there to start speaking a language than to familiarize yourself with its alphabet? Table 1-1 shows you all the letters as well as how each one sounds. Note that there are only 21 letters in the Italian alphabet: missing are *j, k, w, x,* and *y* (which have crept into some Italian words now used in Italy, such as the words **kiwi** and **yogurt**).

TABLE 1-1 Alfabeto (ahl-fah-*beh*-toh)

Letter	Pronunciation	Letter	Pronunciation	Letter	Pronunciation
a	ah	h	*ahk*-kah	q	kooh
b	bee	i	ee	r	*ehr*-reh
c	chee	l	*ehl*-leh	s	*ehs*-seh
d	dee	m	*ehm*-meh	t	tee
e	eh	n	*ehn*-neh	u	ooh
f	*ehf*-feh	o	oh	v	vooh
g	jee	p	pee	z	*dzeh*-tah

Vowels

I start with the tough ones: vowels. The sounds aren't that new, but the connection between the written letter and the actual pronunciation in Italian isn't quite the same as it is in English.

Italian has five written vowels: **a, e, i, o,** and **u.** The following sections tell you how to pronounce them. The stress goes on the *italicized* syllable.

The vowel a

In Italian, the letter *a* has just one pronunciation. Think of the sound of the *a* in the English word *father.* The Italian **a** sounds just like that. I transcribe the Italian a as (ah), as in **casa** (*kah*-zah) *(house)* and **sale** (*sah*-leh) *(salt).*

The vowel e

Try to think of the sound in the French word gourmet (you don't pronounce the t). This sound comes very close to the Italian **e.** I transcribe the **e** sound as (eh). For example, **sole** (*soh*-leh) *(sun).*

The vowel i

The Italian **i** is simply pronounced (ee), as in the English word *see.* Here are some examples: **cinema** (*chee*-neh-mah) *(cinema)* and **vita** (*vee*-tah) *(life).*

The vowel o

The Italian **o** is pronounced as in the English *piano* generally. I list the pronunciation as (oh). Try it out on the following words: **domani** (doh-*mah*-nee) *(tomorrow)* and **piccolo** (*peek*-koh-loh) *(little; small).* However, the **o** can also sound like the o in *off.* The word **botte,** for example, has different meanings *(beating/barrel).*

The vowel u

The Italian **u** sounds always like the English (ooh), as in *zoo.* I use (ooh) to transcribe the Italian **u.** Here are some sample words: **luna** (*looh*-nah) *(moon)* and **frutta** (*frooht*-tah) *(fruit).*

Consonants

Here are some consonants that are pronounced differently in Italian than they are in English.

The consonant c

The Italian **c** has three sounds, depending on which letter follows it:

» **Hard c:** When **c** is followed by **a, o, u,** or any consonant, pronounce it as in the English word *cat.* I transcribe this pronunciation as (k). Examples include **casa** (*kah*-zah) *(house)*, **colpa** (*kohl*-pah) *(fault/guilt)*.

» **Soft c:** When **c** is followed by **e** or **i,** pronounce it as you do the first and last sound in the English word *church.* Examples include **cena** (*cheh*-nah) *(dinner)*, **cibo** (*chee*-boh) *(food)*.

» **Soft sh sound** (as in *shame*): When you have **sc** followed by **e** or **i,** pronounce it like you do in the English word *show.* Examples include **scena** (*sheh*-nah) *(scene)*, and **capisci** (kah-*pee*-shee) *(you understand)*.

This pronunciation scheme sounds terribly complicated, but in the end, it's not that difficult. And it's super important. Here I present it in another way, which you can take as a little memory support:

Follow a scheme like this:

C + i, e = ch

C+ h, o, u, a = k

Sc + i or e = sh

The Italian **g** behaves essentially the same as the **c,** with hard and soft sounds:

G + i, e = g as in **Gina** (*jee*-nah) and **gelato** (geh-*lah*-toh) *(ice-cream*, sort of)

G + h, o, u, a = g as in **spaghetti** (spah-*ghet*-tee) *(spaghetti)*, **gondola** (*gohn*-doh-lah) *(a type of boat in Venice)*, **figura** (fee-*gooh*-rah) *(figure)*, and **gala** (*gah*-lah).

The consonant **h** is *always* silent! It appears in some forms of the verb **avere** (ah-*veh*-reh) *(to have)*, such as **io ho** (*ee*-oh oh), **tu hai** (tooh i), and some words of foreign origin, such as **hobby** (*ohb*-bee).

Consonant clusters

Certain consonant clusters have special sounds in Italian: it's important to get these down as well. Here are a couple to get you started:

>> **gn** is pronounced as the English *ny* sound in canyon. You may already know the Italian words **gnocchi** (*nyohk*-kee) (a delicious dumpling type of pasta) and **signora** (see-*nyoh*-rah) *(Mrs.)*.

>> **gl** is pronounced in the back of the throat like the English word *million* in words like **gli** (lyee) (*the*, masc. pl.) and **famiglia** (fah-*mee*-lyah) *(family)*.

Don't ever say anything like the English **g as in glamour** with the **gl** consonant cluster.

Stressing words properly

Stress is the audible accent that you put on a syllable as you speak it. One syllable always gets more stress than all the others.

Some words give you a hint as to where to stress them because they have an accent on the last syllable. Only vowels have accents. Here are some examples with the stressed syllable italicized:

>> **caffè** (kahf-*feh*) *(coffee)*

>> **città** (cheet-*tah*) *(city)*

>> **perché** (pehr-*keh*) *(why)*

>> **però** (peh-*roh*) *(but)*

>> **università** (ooh-nee-vehr-see-*tah*) *(university)*

With words that do not have an accent mark, you are left on your own to figure out where to place the stress. A good rule of thumb is to place the stress on the penultimate (second-to-last syllable). But there are too many exceptions and rules to list them all here! When in doubt, and you have a burning desire to know — check the dictionary or ask your handy AI app how to pronounce something. Here are a few examples:

>> **melanzane** (meh-lahn-*zah*-neh) *(eggplant)*
>> **bambino** (bahm-*bee*-noh) *(baby)*

But . . .

>> **macchina** (*mahk*-kee-nah) *(car)* (here, the stress is on the first syllable)

Addressing Folks: Greetings and Salutations

The first step toward communicating meaningfully involves being able to greet someone, introduce yourself, and employ some polite conventions, such as please and thank you!

The Italian language clearly recognizes and requires two different conventions of address, formal and informal, depending on whom you're addressing and also the situation. When you understand what convention to use, you're better equipped to interact and to also show regard for cultural differences.

REMEMBER

Formal and informal usage distinctions inform your use of everything from possessive adjectives to verbs in all tenses. You can't get away from this convention — but of course, it's okay to make mistakes!

Formal greetings

Use the following formal phrases when you want to meet and greet a stranger, someone whom you don't know very well, and/or someone to whom you should show respect.

Table 1-2 provides you with some terms generally associated with greetings and salutations. As you go through this table, make a mental note of some of the differences and similarities — there is some overlap — between Table 1-2 and Table 1-3 (in the next section), which provides the informal phrases.

TABLE 1-2 Formal Greetings and Salutations

Italian	English
Buon giorno/Buongiorno	Hello/Good morning/Goodbye
Salve	Hello
Buona sera/Buonasera	Hello/Goodbye/Good evening
Buona notte/Buonanotte	Good night
Signorina	Miss (young woman)
Signora	Mrs./Ma'am (older married or unmarried woman)
Signore	Mr./Sir
Mi chiamo . . .	My name is . . .
Come si chiama?	What's your name?
Come sta?	How are you?
Bene.	Well.
Molto bene.	Very well.
Così così.	So-so.
Abbastanza bene.	Fair/pretty well.
(Sto) male.	(I'm) not well.
Grazie, e Lei?* Note that **Lei** means both *you* formal and *she*; it depends on context!	Thank you, and you?
Di dov'è?	Where are you from?
Sono di . . .	I'm from . . .
Piacere (di conoscerLa).	Nice to meet you.
Molto piacere.	It's a great pleasure.
Arrivederci.	Goodbye.
A dopo/Ci vediamo.	See you later.
A presto.	See you soon.
A domani.	See you tomorrow.
Buona giornata.	Have a good day.
Buona serata.	Have a good evening.

REMEMBER

You use **buona notte!** when you know it's actually bedtime, and you're taking leave; consider it another way of saying, *"(Goodbye and) Sleep well!"* Start to use **buona sera** in the late afternoon until you go to bed.

Informal greetings

The informal is usually designated with the pronouns **tu/voi** (*you sing. and pl.*) and the formal with **Lei** (*you*). You usually use the informal address with family members, friends, pets, people your same age (if you're on the younger side), and children. Refer to Table 1-3 for greetings and salutations.

TABLE 1-3 **Informal Greetings and Salutations**

Italian	English
Ciao!	*Hi!/Bye!*
Come ti chiami?	*What's your name?*
Mi chiamo . . .	*My name is . . .*
Sono . . .	*I'm (meaning My name is . . .)*
Come stai?	*How are you?*
Bene.	*Well.*
Molto bene.	*Very well.*
Così così.	*So-so.*
Male.	*Not well.*
Non c'è male.	*Not bad.*
Grazie, e tu?	*Thank you, and you?*
Piacere (di conoscerti)!	*It's a pleasure (to meet you!)*
Di dove sei?	*Where are you from?*
Sono di . . .	*I'm from . . .*
Che piacere vederti!	*How nice it is to see you!*
Come va?	*How's it going?*

Italian	English
Che c'è di nuovo?	*What's new?*
Niente.	*Nothing.*
Ci vediamo/A dopo.	*See you later.*
A presto.	*See you soon.*
A domani.	*See you tomorrow.*
Buona giornata.	*Have a good day.*
Buona serata.	*Have a good evening.*

TIP

A general rule is that you use the informal when on a first name basis with someone.

Forms of courtesy

It's always good to know how to be courteous when communicating with others. Table 1-4 lists common forms of courtesy.

TABLE 1-4 Being Polite

Italian	English
Per favore/per piacere	*Please*
Grazie.	*Thank you.*
Grazie mille.	*Thanks so much.*
Molte grazie.	*Thank you very much.*
Grazie, molto gentile.	*Thank you, that's very kind (of you).*
Prego.	*You're welcome.*
Mi scusi/Scusi (formal)	*Excuse me./I'm sorry.*
Mi scusi, un'informazione, per favore.	*Excuse me, I need some information, please.*
Scusa/Scusami (informal)	*Excuse me./I'm sorry.*
Mi dispiace.	*I'm sorry.*

Prego not only means *You're welcome*. It also means, *Please, come this way*; *Please, by all means, you first*; or *Here you go!*

When referring to someone, and also when addressing someone directly with their title, cut off the final e when using a last name with masculine titles:

» **Signore** becomes **Signor Tarroni**.

» **Dottore** becomes **Dottor Costa**.

» **Professore** becomes **Professor Gambi**.

The title *Ms.* doesn't exist in Italian, so you use either **Signora** *(Miss)* or **Signorina** *(Mrs./Ma'am)*.

For female professional titles of doctor and professor, you use **Dottoressa** and **Professoressa**.

Using Everyday Numbers

You use numbers all the time, in any language. If you say that you've seen ten movies, you're using a cardinal number. If you say that you're in the tenth grade, you're using an ordinal number. Here I walk you through cardinal and ordinal numbers in Italian.

Counting items with cardinal numbers

When written in full, cardinal numbers are invariable in Italian (except for the number *one*, which can also be an indefinite article; see Chapter 2). Starting with 21, you encounter a neat pattern that you then repeat from 30 to 99.

Following are the numbers from 0 through 29:

» **zero** (0)

» **uno** (1)

» **due** (2)

» **tre** (3)

» **quattro** (4)

» **cinque** (5)

» **sei** (6)

» **sette** (7)

» **otto** (8)

» **nove** (9)

» **dieci** (10)

» **undici** (11)

» **dodici** (12)

» **tredici** (13)

» **quattordici** (14)	» **ventidue** (22)
» **quindici** (15)	» **ventitré** (23)*
» **sedici** (16)	» **ventiquattro** (24)
» **diciassette** (17)	» **venticinque** (25)
» **diciotto** (18)	» **ventisei** (26)
» **diciannove** (19)	» **ventisette** (27)
» **venti** (20)	» **ventotto** (28)
» **ventuno** (21)	» **ventinove** (29)

Except for the word **tre,** all numbers ending in 3 carry an accent, such as **duecentotrè** (203) and **sessantatrè** (63).

REMEMBER

Table 1-5 lists multiples of 10 and 100.

TABLE 1-5 ## Cardinal Numbers with Double and Triple Digits

Multiples of 10	Multiples of 100
dieci (10)	**cento** (100)
venti (20)	**duecento** (200)
trenta (30)	**trecento** (300)
quaranta (40)	**quattrocento** (400)
cinquanta (50)	**cinquecento** (500)
sessanta (60)	**seicento** (600)
settanta (70)	**settecento** (700)
ottanta (80)	**ottocento** (800)
novanta (90)	**novecento** (900)

In Italian, 1,000 is **mille.**

A common error for speakers of English is to say **un mille** for *a thousand/one thousand* — rather, you just say **mille:**

WARNING

> **Vengono mille persone al concerto.** *(A/One thousand people are coming to the concert.)*

Another common error is to use the English convention of pairing the first two numbers with centuries. In English, to say 1929, you group the numbers and say *nineteen twenty-nine*, but in Italian, you say it as one word: **millenovecentoventinove.**

The plural of **mille** is **mila.**

To form higher numbers, you use — **mila** as follows: **duemila** (2,000), **cinquemila** (5,000), and so on.

Here's an example of how you talk about money in Italian. The plural of **euro** in Italian is **euro** — it's invariable:

> **Una Ferari costa duecentosessantanovemila euro.**
> *(A Ferrari costs 269,000 euros.)*

Putting items in order with ordinal numbers

With ordinal numbers, you set things in order, using them to establish ranking, and also to talk about centuries. They behave like adjectives in that they have to agree in gender and number with the nouns or pronouns they are modifying. The first ten have special forms (here they are in the masculine singular):

- » **primo** (1st)
- » **secondo** (2nd)
- » **terzo** (3rd)
- » **quarto** (4th)
- » **quinto** (5th)

- » **sesto** (6th)
- » **settimo** (7th)
- » **ottavo** (8th)
- » **nono** (9th)
- » **decimo** (10th)

You form ordinal numbers beyond **decimo** by dropping the final vowel form the cardinal number and then adding -**esimo,** -**esima, -esimi, -esime** (according to the gender and number). The following are some ordinal numbers from 11th to 20th, in the masculine and feminine and singular and plural forms. They follow the same pattern:

- » **undicesimo, undicesima, undicesimi, undicesime** (11th)
- » **dodicesimo, dodicesima, dodicesimi, dodicesime** (12th)
- » **quattordicesimo** (14th)
- » **sedicesimo** (16th)

>> **diciottesimo** (18th)

>> **ventesimo** (20th)

TIP

When you use an ordinal number in the context of a sentence, you usually place it before the word it refers to, accompanied by the article:

Lei è la sua terza moglie. *(She's his third wife.)*

Using the Calendar

Knowing how to create and handle information about dates is important knowledge to have at your fingertips. Here, I explore the days of the week and months.

Expressing the days of the week

You can use **Che giorno è (oggi)?** to mean *What day of the week is it (today)?* You answer with something like **Oggi è venerdì** *(Today is Friday)*.

You don't capitalize the days of the week in Italian. They're all masculine and take **il**, except for **la domenica** *(Sunday)*:

>> **lunedì** *(Monday)*

>> **martedì** *(Tuesday)*

>> **mercoledì** *(Wednesday)*

>> **giovedì** *(Thursday)*

>> **venerdì** *(Friday)*

>> **sabato** *(Saturday)*

>> **domenica** *(Sunday)*

Other important words to add to your temporal toolbox (for now) include the following:

>> **giorno** *(day)*

>> **oggi** *(today)*

>> **domani** *(tomorrow)*

>> **il fine settimana/il week-end** *(the weekend)*

>> **anno** *(year)*

>> **mese** *(month)*

>> **settimana** *(week)*

You generally use the definite article with days of the week *only* when you're talking about a repeated action. For example, compare the following two sentences:

Il venerdì sera esco sempre con Emilia. *(On Friday evenings, I always go out with Emilia.)*

Venerdì sera esco con Emilia. *(On Friday evening, I am going out with Emilia.)*

Managing your calendar

Italy shares the same calendar as the rest of the world. The following sections give you the vocabulary that you can use to talk about **secoli** *(centuries)*, **anni** *(years)*, **stagioni** *(seasons)*, **mesi** *(months)*, and **date** *(dates)*.

When you need to say "in a certain year," use the preposition **in**, combined with the article **il**, forming **nel**, like this:

nel 1945 (millenovecentoquarantacinque) *(in 1945)*

As in Vivaldi's *Le quattro stagioni*, the four seasons are **la primavera** *(spring)*, **l'estate** *(summer)*, **l'autunno** *(fall/autumn)*, and **l'inverno** *(winter)*.

To see how to talk about weather, see the verb **fare** *(to do or make)* in Chapter 3.

The following sections explore important vocabulary when you're working with months and days, trying to make a date, and figuring out your schedule.

Mesi e date: Months and dates

Just like the days and the seasons, you don't capitalize the months, which follow:

>> **gennaio** *(January)*

>> **febbraio** *(February)*

>> **marzo** *(March)*

>> **aprile** *(April)*

>> **maggio** *(May)*

>> **giugno** *(June)*

>> **luglio** *(July)*

>> **agosto** *(August)*

» **settembre** *(September)*

» **ottobre** *(October)*

» **novembre** *(November)*

» **dicembre** *(December)*

Making a date

When mentioning a particular date, you use cardinal numbers, except for the first of the month, in which case, you use the ordinal number **primo**.

REMEMBER

Word order is important: You write dates in the day-month-year format, without commas. (Unlike the common usage in the United States, which is month-day-year). Refer to these examples:

> **Oggi è il primo maggio.** *(Today is May 1st.)*
>
> **John è nato il cinque settembre duemilacinque.** *(John was born on September 5, 2005.)*
>
> **Partiamo il quindici aprile (il 15/4).** *(We will leave on April 15th/on 4/15.)*

TIP

To ask for today's date, you can usually use one of these two options:

> **Che giorno è?** *(What day is it?/What's the date?)*/**Qual è la data di oggi?** *(What's today's date?)*

To answer, use this structure:

> **Oggi è il ventinove febbraio.** *(Today is February 29th.)*

To find out more about your new Italian friend, you can ask when their birthday is:

> **Quando è il tuo compleanno?** *(When's your birthday?)*
>
> **Il sette novembre.** *(November 7th.)*

Making the Most of Time

If you want to catch a train or a plane, make sure the store is open, or check the movie theater's schedule, you need to know the right time. Here I explain the basics of asking the time and saying at what time something is.

Asking the time

To ask the time, you say:

Che ora è?/Che ore sono? *(What time is it?)*

These two questions are interchangeable.

The answer, however, is not. To respond, you must use the third person singular of the verb **essere** *(to be)* — **è** — with singular time indicators, and the third person plural of the verb **essere** — **sono** — with plural time indicators.

To use the singular form to tell time, follow this pattern for times that start at 1:00, noon, and midnight:

È + l' + una *(It's one o'clock/It's 1:00)*, **È mezzogiorno** *(It's noon/12 p.m.)*, **È mezzanotte** *(It's midnight/12 a.m.)*.

You use **e** *(and)* when giving the minutes past the hour. After you pass the half hour, you generally jump to the next hour and use the word **meno** *(minus)* (hour *minus* minutes):

» **È l'una.** *(It's 1:00.)*/**È l'una e venti.** *(It's 1:20.)*

» **È l'una e un quarto.** *(It's a quarter past 1:00./1:15.)*

» **È l'una meno dieci.** *(It's 10 to 1:00./12:50.)*

» **È l'una e mezzo/a.** *(It's half past 1:00./1:30.)*

To write a plural time, follow this structure:

Sono + le + hour (any time other than 1:00) + **e** or **meno** + a portion of the hour or a number of minutes

Here are some examples:

» **Sono le due e dieci.** *(It's 10 past 2:00./2:10.)*

» **Sono le otto meno un quarto.** *(It's a quarter to 8:00./7:45.)*

» **Sono le quattro e mezza/o.** *(It's half past 4:00./4:30.)*

When using the 12-hour system, you can add **di mattina** *(a.m./in the morning)*, **del pomeriggio** *(p.m./in the afternoon)*, **di sera** *(p.m./in the evening)*, and **di notte** (the hours of the night), to avoid misunderstandings, as in:

> **Balliamo fino alle alle quattro di notte.** *(We dance until 4:00 in the morning.)*

Of course, you can always use the 24-hour clock. This system is much more common in Italy than in the United States. You find the 24-hour system printed on Italian train schedules, event programs, class times, and so forth: **Il treno parte alle [ore] 15:45.** *(The train is leaving at 15:45 [3:45 p.m.].)*

A che ora: saying "at"

To ask *at what time* something begins or ends, you simply say **A che ora** *(at what time?)*. To answer, you use a form of the preposition *at* — **a**, **all'**, or **alle** — in your response:

> **A che ora vai a dormire?** *(At what time do you go to sleep?)*
>
> **A mezzanotte.** *(At midnight.)*

Use the following to create this:

>> **a** with no article: **A mezzogiorno** *(At noon.)* or **A mezzanotte** *(At midnight.)*

>> **all'** only with 1:00: **All'una.** *(At 1:00.)*

>> **alle**: When the hour is plural, (meaning it's later than 1:00): **Alle due.** *(At 2:00.)*

Getting into the Parts of Speech

This section leads you through the building blocks of sentences. Consider these blocks as challenging scaffolding that helps you to construct your sentences, piece by piece. I walk you through gender and number, and introduce verbs, adjectives, adverbs, and prepositions.

Setting up simple sentences

Forming simple sentences is, well, simple. The basic sentence structure of Italian is subject-verb-object — the same as in English. Nouns in Italian are gender specific. In the following example, you can see how this structure works:

Pietro ha una macchina. *(Pietro has a car.)*

Coping with gendered words

You can't get around the use of gender in Italian. Most of the elements that make up a sentence — nouns, definite articles *(the)*, indefinite articles *(a/an)*, contracted prepositions, adjectives, personal pronouns, direct and indirect object pronouns, past participles — must reckon with gender and number — and also follow some basic rules. Chapter 2 goes into detail about the gender and number of nouns, articles, and possessive adjectives.

Luckily, most of this grammar follows some very cool schemata that you can plug in anywhere as soon as you learn the rules (and some exceptions to those rules). Commit them to memory if you can.

Nouns and gender

All nouns have a specific gender (masculine and feminine) and number (singular and plural). Learning the gender of nouns as soon as you encounter them is imperative. Check out Chapter 2, where I explain what you need to know about nouns and gender.

Indefinite articles

An *indefinite article* refers to persons or objects (such as *a dancer* and *an apple*). The indefinite article (see Chapter 2) corresponds to *a/an* (and *one*) in English and is generally a general way to reference something; they are used in a very similar way to their English counterpart. Indefinite articles are only used with singular nouns. There are four different indefinite articles in Italian (**uno, un, un',** and **una**).

Definite articles

A *definite article* is more diverse and specific than an indefinite article and indicates a specific person or thing and agrees with the noun in gender and number. Many times the definite article corresponds to the English usage of the article *the* (such as, *the cake is in the oven*). There are six definite articles in Italian (**l'**, **lo**, **il**, **la**, **gli**, **i**, and **le**). Refer to Chapter 2 for much more on definite articles.

Referring to folks with pronouns

A *pronoun* replaces, as the word itself says, a noun. When you talk about Jim, for example, you can replace his name with *he*. You often use pronouns to avoid repetition.

Several types of pronouns exist. The most important ones for you are the subject pronouns (also called *personal pronouns*), which refer to **io** *(I)*, **tu** *(you* informal), **lui** *(he)*, **lei** *(she)*, **Lei** *(you* formal), **noi** *(we)*, **voi** *(you all)*, and **loro** *(they)*. Every verb form refers to one of these pronouns. See Chapter 3 for more on the subject pronouns and verbs, including preferred pronouns and gender inclusivity.

Introducing regular and irregular verbs

There are so many verbs in Italian! Verbs truly are the glue that bind the different parts of speech together. A *verb* is the part of speech that shows an action or a state of being, and it's generally presented as an infinitive, such as **mangiare** *(to eat)*.

Regular verbs follow a certain pattern in their conjugation, which means that you can predict a regular verb's form in any part of any tense. On the other hand, you can't predict irregular verbs in this way — they behave a bit like individualists. Refer to the Appendix for conjugations of verbs, as well as the verb chapters in this book.

Presenting the simple tenses: present, past, and future

People clearly don't use just one tense. Sometimes you need to report what you did yesterday or outline what you're going to do tomorrow. These three tenses (past, present, and future) aren't high grammar — just basic stuff.

You find more information on some simple tenses in Chapter 3 (present) and Chapter 7 (future), and a compound tense (present perfect) in Chapter 6. Chapter 8 walks you through subjunctive tenses (both simple and compound), the conditional, and the imperative.

Describing with adjectives

An *adjective* is a word that describes a noun — whether a person, a thing, or whatever — with a quality or characteristic. (You can read more about adjectives in Chapter 2.)

Clarifying with adverbs

Adverbs are another important way of enriching language. In Italian, adverbs are invariable, which means that you don't have to worry about making them agree with the words they modify. Chapter 2 examines adverbs in greater detail.

Joining with prepositions

Prepositions are words that you need to link other words in a sentence in order to create fuller sentences. Chapter 4 explores what you need to know about prepositions in Italian.

IN THIS CHAPTER

» Exploring gender

» Clarifying gender with nouns

» Dealing with definite articles

» Keeping things general with indefinite articles

» Possessing with adjectives

» Substituting with object pronouns

Chapter **2**

Determining Gender ABCs

G ender and number are vital parts of the Italian language. Every noun, definite article, indefinite article, adjective, possessive adjective, and object pronoun needs to be in-line with gender. In this chapter, you gain confidence in applying gender to many of the building blocks of the Italian language.

Focusing on Gender

In a Romance language like Italian, nouns are assigned a grammatical category called gender, which means that the nouns are either masculine or feminine, but this has nothing to do with the natural sex of the noun. Because gender classification is somewhat arbitrary, you have to learn the gender of nouns as you encounter them. This concept also applies to the parts of speech related to nouns like articles, pronouns, and adjectives.

Even though Italian grammar dictates that the gender defaults to masculine (such as in dictionaries), even when referring to a room that has, for example, 14 women and 2 men, things are changing slowly in Italy to become more inclusive.

That being said, many people are utilizing Italian in different ways to be inclusive, such as:

>> Using an asterisk **(*)** or a schwa **(ə)** when writing (and speaking) to groups of mixed gender, and also where some participants may identify as nonbinary or whose gender isn't known. This way, they can avoid privileging one gender over the other.

For example, they might start an email with: **Car* tutt*** or **Carə tuttə** instead of the traditional **Cari tutti** *(Dear all)*, which defaults to the masculine.

>> Making the feminine the default gender in the classroom (and explaining why you're doing that), just to mix things up.

For example, **Care tutte** *(Dear all)* and **Se una volesse andare in Italia** . . . *(If one wanted to go to Italy . . .).*

>> Referring to both genders instead of the conventional masculine.

For example, **le mie studentesse e i miei studenti** *(my female students and my male students)* rather than **i miei studenti** for *my students* (which is masculine by default).

>> Recent progressive initiatives in some Italian schools are sensitive to naming, asking students and teachers to choose their preferred pronouns. However, in Italian, you only use **loro/il-la-i-le loro** *(they/theirs)* when you're referring to a plural subject. Chapter 3 discusses pronouns in greater detail.

Engendering Nouns

Nouns are those exciting and diverse basic building blocks that cover every topic under the sun; they refer to people, places, things, or ideas. Nouns serve similar purposes in Italian and English, but there's an important difference that you can't get around: gender. Often, an Italian noun's grammatical gender is merely a product of convention and usage: **il sole** *(sun)* and **il giorno** *(day)* are masculine, but **la luna** *(moon)* and **la notte** *(night)* are feminine.

The following sections delve deeper into the world of nouns and gender, examining masculine and feminine nouns and nouns that are exceptions to the rule.

Distinguishing between masculine and feminine nouns

In most Indo-European languages (the family to which both Italian and English belong), nouns have a gender. In Italian, you deal with two genders: masculine and feminine. Other parts of speech — such as demonstrative pronouns, combined prepositions, articles, and adjectives — reflect noun gender, as well, and these other parts of speech have to agree with the gender of the noun.

This section focuses on nouns, discussing what word endings tell you about gender and providing a map for transforming singular nouns into plural nouns.

Grammatically, the noun endings in the singular usually help you figure out to which gender they belong. You have to watch out for exceptions to the norm, but first things first: the regular guys.

Table 2-1 illustrates the noun endings for masculine and feminine singular and plural nouns. In general, nouns ending in -a are feminine and nouns ending in -o are masculine. Nouns ending in -e are either masculine or feminine, and you need to learn their gender upon first encounter.

TABLE 2-1 **Regular Singular and Plural Noun Endings**

Gender	Singular	Plural
Masculine	-o	-i
Feminine	-a	-e
Masculine or feminine	-e	-i

TIP

Some nouns end in -ore in the masculine and -ice in the feminine, such as these:

Masculine	Feminine
attore *(actor)*	**attrice** *(actress)*
pittore *(male painter)*	**pittrice** *(female painter)*

You add an **h** to the plurals of nouns ending in -**ca**, -**co**, -**go**, and -**ga,** to keep the hard sound of *k* or *g*, such as with the word **amica** *(female friend)* to create **amiche** *(female friends)*, **fuoco** *(fire)* to create **fuochi** *(fires)*, **lago** *(lake)* to create **laghi** *(lakes)*, and **targa** *(license plate)* to create **targhe** *(license plates)*. One word that doesn't follow this spelling and pronunciation exception is the plural form of **amico** *(male friend)*, which is **amici** *(male friends)*. I have no clue why it does that!

Masculine nouns

Masculine nouns often end in -**o** in the singular and -**i** in the plural, like those here:

Singular	Plural
biscotto *(cookie)*	**biscotti** *(cookies)*
libro *(book)*	**libri** *(books)*
amico *(friend)*	**amici** *(friends)*
giorno *(day)*	**giorni** *(days)*
ragazzo *(boy)*	**ragazzi** *(boys)*

Some masculine nouns end in -**e** in the singular and in -**i** in the plural, such as with these very common nouns:

Singular	Plural
ristorante *(restaurant)*	**ristorante** *(restaurants)*
esame *(exam)*	**esami** *(exams)*
padre *(father)*	**padri** *(fathers)*
bicchiere *(glass,* as in glass of water)	**bicchieri** *(glasses)*
studente *(student)*	**studenti** *(students)*
mare *(sea)*	**mari** *(seas)*

Some nouns ending in -**a** in the singular and -**i** in the plural are masculine because they derive from classical Greek:

Singular	Plural
un problema (a or one problem)	**due problemi** (two problems)
un tema (a or one theme)	**due temi** (two themes)
un programma (a program or plan)	**molti programmi** (many programs or plans)

Feminine nouns

Feminine nouns often end in **-a** in the singular and **-e** in the plural. Note these examples:

Singular	Plural
ora (hour)	**ore** (hours)
pasta (pastry)	**paste** (pastries)
pizza (pizza)	**pizze** (pizzas)
ragazza (girl)	**ragazze** (girls)
macchina (car)	**macchine** (cars)
studentessa (female student)	**studentesse** (female students)
amica (female friend)	**amiche** (female friends)
donna (woman)	**donne** (women)

REMEMBER

The noun **pasta** has different meanings depending on the context. It can mean *pasta* (such as a dish of spaghetti), as well as *pastry* (a baked good), and the *dough* you use to make the pastry, pasta, and bread. Don't confuse the word **pasta** with **pasto**, which means *meal*.

Some feminine nouns, like masculine nouns, end in **-e** in the singular and in **-i** in the plural. Here's a good hint for remembering that some of these words are feminine when they end in **-ione** in the singular. Note these two examples:

Singular	Plural
una lezione (one lesson)	**due lezioni** (two lessons)
una regione (one region)	**tre regioni** (three regions)

Noting exceptions

Some nouns have exceptions when ending in a consonant or an accented final vowel, when using an abbreviated form, and when the word is borrowed from another language. Hence, you need to be able to identify the gender of these exceptions.

Masculine nouns may also end in a consonant in the singular. These words are often borrowed from another language, and they're *invariable,* which means they have the exact same form in the singular and in the plural.

Here, I illustrate these invariable nouns that end in a consonant. With these words, articles come in very handy, as I discuss in the two sections, "Specifying with Definite Articles" and "Generalizing with Indefinite Articles" later in this chapter.

Singular	Plural
un autobus *(a/one bus)*	**due autobus** *(two buses)*
uno sport *(a/one sport)*	**tre sport** *(three sports)*
un bar *(a/one bar/cafe)*	**quattro bar** *(four bars/cafes)*
uno chef *(a/one chef)*	**cinque chef** *(five chefs)*

When you see the indefinite article **uno** (meaning *a, an,* or *one*) preceding a noun, how do you know whether it means *one* or *a/an?* Let context and common sense be your guide when in doubt.

Two important Italian masculine nouns have an accented final vowel (which means that they're invariable):

Singular	Plural
un caffè *(a coffee)*	**otto caffè** *(eight coffees)*
un lunedì *(a Monday)*	**nove lunedì** *(nine Mondays)*

Three types of invariable nouns include the following:

>> Nouns that end in an accented final vowel, such as **un caffè** *(a café)* and **una città** *(a city)*. Other common feminine nouns of this type are **una virtù** *(a virtue)*, **una verità** *(a truth)*, and **un'università** *(a university)*.

>> Nouns that end in a consonant (these are rare!), such as **bar** *(bar)*, **film** *(film/movie)*, and **computer** *(computer)*. These nouns are all masculine.

>> Nouns that are abbreviations, such as **zoo**, masc. *(zoo)*, **bici,** fem. *(bicycle)*, **radio,** fem. *(radio)*, and **cinema,** masc. *(cinema/ movie-house)*.

Note these very common exceptions of irregular masculine plural nouns:

Singular	Plural
un uomo *(a/one man)*	**cinque uomini** *(five men)*
un cinema *(a/one cinema)*	**due cinema** *(two cinemas)*
uno zoo *(one zoo)*	**due zoo** *(two zoos)*
un frigo *(one fridge)*	**tre frigo** *(three fridges)*

The following shows a few exceptions to the general rules governing number and gender with feminine nouns. Most are abbreviations. Look to the definite article for a dead giveaway concerning gender.

Singular	Plural
un'auto *(a/one car;* from **automobile**)	**due auto** *(two cars)*
una mano *(a/one hand)*	**due mani** *(two hands)*
una moto *(a/one motorcycle;* from **motociclette**)	**due moto** *(two motorcycles)*

Many words for body parts have irregular plurals, such as **mano/mani** *(hand/hands)* and **braccio/braccia** *(arm/arms)*.

REMEMBER

Nouns that end in **–ista** have three forms: one identical singular form for both masculine and feminine, and then both a masculine and a feminine plural. The following shows some examples:

Singular	Masc Plural	Fem Plural
l'artista *(artist,* m/f)	**gli artisti** *(male artists),*	**le artiste** *(female artists)*
il/la pianista *(pianist,* m/f)	**i pianisti** *(male pianists),*	**le pianiste** *(female pianists)*
il/la barista *(barista,* m/f)	**i baristi** *(male baristas),*	**le bariste** *(female baristas)*

Sorting out Definite and Indefinite Articles

Italian, like English, has both definite and indefinite articles — *the* and *a/an*, respectively.

An *indefinite article* refers to persons or objects (such as *a dancer* and *an apple*). The indefinite article corresponds to *a/an* (and *one*) in English and is generally a general way to reference something; they're used in a very similar way to their English counterpart. Indefinite articles are always singular and are only used with singular nouns. Consequently, Italian indefinite articles agree in gender. There are four different indefinite articles in Italian (**uno, un, un', una**).

A *definite article* is more diverse and specific than an indefinite article and indicates a specific person or thing. Many times the definite article corresponds to the English usage of the article *the* (such as, *the cake is in the oven*). Definite articles agree in gender and number with singular and plural nouns, and so are both singular and plural. There are six definite articles in Italian (**l', lo, il, la, gli, i, le**).

With the definite article, you point to a specific item:

Il bambino è caduto dall'altalena. *(The child fell off the swing.)*

With the indefinite article, you point to one thing among many like things:

Leggi un libro? *(Are you reading a book?)*

Memorizing new nouns with their articles can help you remember the nouns' genders, as well.

TIP

In the following sections, you can dive into the articles that frequently accompany nouns and that must agree with (or match) them.

Specifying and using the definite articles

Because a clear and reliable indicator of a noun's gender is the definite article, I focus first on them. Definite articles, which translate as the word *the*, frequently accompany nouns much more than in English usage, and agree with nouns in number and gender. For example, in order to say *Italy is beautiful*, **L'Italia è bella**, you use the article **l'** (whereas in English you don't).

In Italian, articles vary in gender, number, and spelling:

> **Il libro è sul tavolo.** *(The book is on the table.)*

> **I bambini stanno giocando in giardino.** *(The children are playing in the garden.)*

In Table 2-2, I show you which definite articles to use with the specific types of masculine nouns. Italian has three forms of the singular masculine definite article: **il, lo,** and **l'**, which you use with singular nouns. Italian has two forms of plural definite articles, **i** and **gli**, that you use with plural masculine nouns. Commit them to memory if you can.

TABLE 2-2 Masculine Definite Articles

Placement	Singular	Singular Examples	Plural	Plural Examples
Before most single consonants and groups of consonants	il	**il ragazzo** *(the boy)* **il bar** *(the bar)*	i	**i ragazzi** *(boys)* **i bar** *(the bars)*
Before **gn-, pn-, ps-, s** + another consonant, **x-, y-,** and **z-**	lo	**lo gnocco** *(the dumpling)* **lo studente** *(the male student)* **lo zaino** *(the backpack)*	gli	**gli gnocchi** *(the dumplings)* **gli studenti** *(the male students)* **gli zaini** *(the backpacks)*
Before any vowel	l'	**l'uomo** *(the man)* **l'amico** *(the male friend)*	gli	**gli uomini** *(the men)* **gli amici** *(the male friends)*

Table 2-3 lists the two forms of the definite article used with singular feminine nouns, **la** and **l'**, as well as the plural feminine article, which has only one form: **le**.

TABLE 2-3 Feminine Definite Articles

Placement	Singular	Singular Example	Plural	Plural Example
Before any consonant or group of consonants	la	**la casa** *(the house)* **la mela** *(the apple)*	le	**le case** *(the houses)* **le mele** *(the apples)*
Before any vowel	l'	**l'amica** *(the female friend)* **l'ora** *(the hour)*	le	**le amiche** *(the female friends)* **le ore** *(the hours)*

Knowing when (and when not) to use a definite article

REMEMBER

Deciding when and when not to use the definite article is a tricky topic in Italian. Italian uses the definite article much more than English. And it doesn't always translate as the word *the*! For example, Italian uses articles before the following:

>> Foods: **Amo il pane.** *(I love bread.)*; **Mangio le mele.** *(I eat apples.)*

>> Dates: **il 25 aprile** *(April 25)*

>> Titles (when talking about someone, not with direct address): **il professor Baldini** *(Professor Baldini)*

>> Abstract nouns: such as **la forza** *(strength)* and **l'amore** *(love)*

>> Concrete nouns: **Il cibo è necessario.** *(Food is necessary.)*

>> Possessive adjectives: **la mia borsa** *(my bag)*

Here, I discuss when you need to use a definite article in Italian for people, places, and things.

People

In Italian, you use articles when talking about a professional or before a female name to express affection and familiarity

(**La Elena**), but you don't use them in direct address. For example, you use the article when you say

> **Ho visto il dottor Cecconi martedì sera.** *(I saw Dr. Cecconi on Tuesday evening.)*

But you don't use it when you say

> **Buon giorno, dottor Cecconi.** *(Good morning, Dr. Cecconi.)*

Places

You use the Italian definite article with the following geographical features:

» Mountains, rivers, and lakes: **le Alpi** *(the Alps)*, **il Po** *(the Po River)*, and so on

» Many large islands and archipelagos: **la Sicilia** *(Sicily)*, **le Hawaii** *(Hawaii)*, and so on

» Regions and states: **il Lazio** *(the Lazio region)*, **la California** *(California)*, and so on

» Nations (singular or plural) and continents: **l'Italia** *(Italy)*, **Gli Stati Uniti** *(the United States)*, and so on

Things

You use the definite article with the following things:

» Countable plural nouns: **I gatti e i cani sono i nostri amici.** *(Cats and dogs are our friends.)*

» Uncountable nouns: **il sale** *(salt)*, **lo zucchero** *(sugar)*, **l'acqua** *(water)*, **l'amore** *(love)*, **la pazienza** *(patience)*, and so on

Generalizing with indefinite articles

Corresponding to the English *a* or *an*, Italian uses the indefinite articles **un, un', una,** and **uno.** You use them only with singular nouns, as in **un paese** *(a/one town or country)*. Table 2-4 lays out the forms of the indefinite article used with singular masculine nouns.

TABLE 2-4 **Masculine Indefinite Articles**

Article	Placement	Examples
un	Before any vowel or consonant and most groups of consonants	**un amico** *(a friend)* **un treno** *(a train)*
uno	Before **gn-**, **pn-**, **ps-**, **s** + another consonant, **x-**, **y-**, and **z-**	**uno psicologo** *(a male psychologist)* **uno studente** *(a male student)* **uno zio** *(an uncle)*

Table 2-5 spells out the forms of the indefinite article used with singular feminine nouns.

TABLE 2-5 **Feminine Indefinite Articles**

Article	Placement	Examples
una	Before any consonant or group of consonants	**una casa** *(a house)* **una strega** *(a witch)* **una lezione** *(a lesson)*
un'	Before any vowel	**un'ora** *(an hour)*

TIP

You use the indefinite article **uno** with the exact same set of words with which you use the singular definite article **lo**. See the following word sets from left to right to see this in action:

uno zaino *(a backpack)*	**lo zaino** *(the backpack)*
uno stadio *(a stadium)*	**lo stadio** *(the stadium)*
uno psicologo *(a psychologist)*	**lo psicologo** *(the psychologist)*

Possessing with Possessive Adjectives

When you want to denote ownership or possession while referring to someone or something, to say *my/mine*, you use the possessive adjective. The main difference between possessives in English and Italian is that the Italian possessives absolutely must agree in number and in gender with what's being possessed.

The following tells you how to match the Italian possessives to the nouns to which they refer and how you can make something possessive, and introduces you to the vocabulary associated with family members.

Forming possessives

The formula for possessive adjectives, when not talking about exceptions to rules, is as follows:

> Definite article (il/la/i/le) + Possessive adjective (one of four forms) + Noun

Note how each possessive adjective in this list of examples follows the formula, agrees with the noun being possessed, and precedes the noun:

» **il mio professore** *(my professor)*

» **la mia penna** *(my pen)*

» **i miei professori** *(my professors)*

» **le mie penne** *(my pens)*

WARNING

Unlike in the English *his/her*, in the third-person singular Italian **il suo/la sua/i suoi/le sue** *(his/her)* the possessive adjective doesn't convey whether the owner is male or female. That information is clarified only by the context of the sentence; for example, **la sua barca** can mean *his boat* or *her boat*. The context lets you know that you're saying *his boat*: **Davide porta la sua barca in Croazia.** *(Davide is taking his boat to Croatia.)*

In other words, possessive adjectives must agree in number and gender with the noun they're modifying:

Jenny ha portato i suoi sci. *(Jenny brought her skis.)*

Table 2-6 lists possessive adjectives and possessive pronouns, along with the corresponding definite articles.

TABLE 2-6 Possessive Adjectives and Pronouns

Translation	Masculine Singular	Masculine Plural	Feminine Singular	Feminine Plural
my/mine	il mio	i miei	la mia	le mie
your/yours (sing.)	il tuo	i tuoi	la tua	le tue
his/hers/its *your/yours* (formal)	il suo	i suoi	la sua	le sue
our/ours	il nostro	i nostri	la nostra	le nostre
your/yours (pl.)	il vostro	i vostri	la vostra	le vostre
their/theirs	il loro	i loro	la loro	le loro

REMEMBER

What's different about **loro**? The possessive adjective **loro** *(their)* doesn't change or agree, regardless of the noun. The only indicator of the gender and number of the noun is the definite article, which is *always* used with **loro** (even with singular family relatives: see the section "Using possessive adjectives with family" later in this chapter).

Using the preposition di

In English, you assign ownership by simply adding an apostrophe and the letter *s* (or just the apostrophe), as in *Maria's cat*. In Italian, that same phrase becomes **Il gatto di Maria** (literally, *the cat of Maria*).

TIP

You never use an apostrophe to denote ownership in Italian.

In Italian, you have some options to express possession. Context and intent can guide you in deciding which option is more appropriate for each situation:

>> Add a possessive adjective to what's being possessed:

il suo gatto *(his/her cat)*

>> Introduce the owner by using the preposition **di** *(of)*:

l'università di Lilly *(Lilly's university)*; **il cibo della mensa** *(the dining hall's food)*

Contract the **di** if necessary. See Chapter 4 for more on when and how to combine **di** + a definite article when it precedes a noun.

TIP

Using possessive adjectives with family

In order to talk about possession within a family unit, you need to know some vocabulary associated with family members:

>> **la madre** *(mother)*

>> **il padre** *(father)*

>> **la mamma** *(mom/mommy)*

>> **il papà** *(pop/dad/daddy)*, **il babbo** *(dad, daddy;* in some regions)

>> **i genitori** *(parents)*

>> **la sorella** *(sister)*, **le sorelle** *(sisters)*

>> **il fratello** *(brother)*, **i fratelli** *(brothers/siblings)*

>> **il marito** *(husband)*

>> **la moglie** *(wife)*

>> **il nonno** *(grandfather)*, **la nonna** *(grandmother)*, **i nonni** *(grandparents)*

>> **la zia** *(aunt)*, **lo zio** *(uncle)*, **gli zii** *(aunts and uncles)*

>> **la cugina** *(cousin,* f), **il cugino** *(cousin,* m), **i cugini** *(cousins)*

>> **il figlio** *(son)*, **la figlia** *(daughter)*, **i figli** *(children/sons)*

>> **il nipote** *(nephew/grandson)*, **la nipote** *(niece/granddaughter)*, **i nipoti** *(nieces and nephews/nephews/grandsons/grandchildren)*, **le nipoti** *(nieces and granddaughters)*

The words **nipote/nipoti** seem almost problematic in their catchall versatility, so keep context in mind, use the gender- and number-specific definite article, and add a clarification when necessary. For example:

TIP

Mia nipote Maria (la figlia di mia sorella) studia a Lecce queto semestre. *(My niece Maria (my sister's daughter) is studying in Lecce this semester.)*

When using possessive adjectives with singular family members, remember that you *never* use the definite article, but you must use it with plural family members.

So, you'd say the following:

>> **mio fratello** *(my brother)* but **i miei fratelli** *(my brothers/ my siblings)*

>> **tua zia** *(your aunt)* but **le tue zie** *(your aunts)*

>> **sua cugina** (*his/her cousin,* fem.) but **le sue cugine** (*his/her cousins,* fem.)

Except for **loro**, which is invariable, where you must always use an article:

la loro sorella *(their sister)* and **le loro sorelle** *(their sisters)*

Except for a few exceptions, which also take an article: **la mia mamma** (but **mia madre/***my* mother), **il mio papà**, and **il mio babbo** (but **mio padre/***my father*).

Considering body parts and clothing

When you talk about body parts and clothing, in Italian, you generally don't use a possessive adjective (whereas you do in English). Frequently, you accompany this vocabulary with reflexive verbs (see Chapter 3 for more on those types of verbs).

Here are some examples:

>> **farsi male a** *(to hurt one's)*
Mi sono fatta male al polpaccio. *(I've hurt my calf.)*

>> **fare male** *(to hurt)*
Mi fa male la testa. *(My head hurts.)*

>> **mettersi** *(to wear, to put on)*
Mi metto le lenti a contatto prima di uscire. *(I put on my contact lenses before going out.)*

Knowing when the possessive pronoun is enough

Use possessive pronouns to refer to something already mentioned or implied. Possessive pronouns agree in number and gender with whatever they're substituting. Sometimes, you use the possessive pronouns to emphasize ownership:

> **Questo è il mio problema, non il tuo.** *(This is my problem, not yours.)*

Enriching Your Sentences with Object Pronouns

Sometimes it's better to refer to an object that's already been mentioned or implied by substituting it with a pronoun, instead of repeating the noun all over again.

In this section, I introduce direct and indirect object pronouns and show you how to substitute direct and indirect objects with their pronouns. The object pronouns precede the verb, unless you're using them in a command (see Chapter 8).

Dealing with direct object pronouns

A *direct object pronoun* substitutes a direct object and agrees in gender and number with that object. A direct object answers the question "Who?" or "What?"

Consider these examples:

> **Conosci Francesca?** *(Do you know Francesca?)*
>
> **Sì, la conosco.** *(Yes, I know her.)*
>
> **No, non la conosco.** *(No, I do not know her.)*

Here you can use the direct object pronoun **la** *(her)*, instead of repeating the direct object (Francesca):

> **Leggi il libro?** *(Are you reading the book?)*
>
> **Sì, lo leggo.** *(Yes, I'm reading it.)*

In this question, *the book* is the direct object. In order to say *Yes, I am reading it*, you have to replace *the book* with the masculine singular direct object pronoun **lo**.

The third person of the direct object pronoun can either mean *it* (fem. or masc.), *him*, or *her*, depending on context:

> **Vedi ancora Stefano? Sì, lo vedo.** *(Do you still see Stefano? Yes, I see him.)*

> **Dove prendete il taxi? Lo prendiamo alla stazione.** *(Where are you all getting the cab? We're getting it at the station.)*

> **Capisci la prof? La capisco.** *(Do you understand the professor? Yes, I understand her.)*

> **Mangi la carne? Non la mangio più.** *(Do you eat meat? I don't eat it anymore.)*

Here's a more common usage of these direct object pronouns in everyday speech:

> **Giancarlo, mi senti?** *(Giancarlo do/can you hear me?)*

> **Si, ti sento!** *(Yes, I hear you.)*

REMEMBER

The word **ecco** *(Here you go!/Here it is!)* is frequently used with direct object pronouns. **Ecco** is used only when pointing something out, and a direct object pronoun can be attached to **ecco** to refer to the object being pointed out. Check out these examples:

> **Dov'è la mia altra scarpa?** *(Where's my other shoe?)*

> **Eccola!** *(Here it is!)*

> **Gigio, dove sei?** *(Gigio, where are you?)*

> **Eccomi!** *(Here I am!)*

> **Dove sono i bambini?** *(Where are the children?)*

> **Eccoli!** *(Here they are!)*

Coping with indirect object pronouns

An indirect object answers the question "To whom?" An indirect object pronoun replaces an indirect object, generally indicated in

Italian by the preposition **a** *(to)*. Indirect object pronouns must also be used with the verb *piacere (to like)* (see Chapter 3):

Scrivi alla nonna? *(Are you writing to grandma?)*

Sì, le scrivo dopo cena. *(Yes, I'll write to her after dinner.)*

In this example, the feminine singular indirect object pronoun **le** substitutes *to grandma (to her)*. Here's an example:

Dici la verità al babbo? *(Are you going to tell dad the truth?)*

You have to replace *to dad* with the masculine singular indirect object pronoun **gli.**

Here's one more example using the indirect objects **mi** and **ti:**

Anna, mi dai una mano? *(Anna, will you give me a hand?)*

Certo, ti do una mano volentieri. *(Of course, I'll gladly give you a hand.)*

Choosing the Proper Pronouns

Check out Table 2-7, where I conveniently place all the personal (or subject), direct object, and indirect object pronouns, so you can reference them as you need them, and also so you can see how they align and compare to each other. Try to commit this table to memory.

TABLE 2-7 Pronouns

	Personal Pronouns	Direct Object Pronouns	Indirect Object Pronouns
First-person singular	**io**	mi	mi
Second-person singular	**tu**	ti	ti
Third-person singular	**lui/lei/Lei**	**lo/la/La**	**gli/le/Le**
First-person plural	**noi**	ci	ci
Second-person plural	**voi**	vi	vi
Third-person plural	**loro/Loro**	li/le	**gli/loro/Loro**

The third person singular **lei/Lei**, **la/La** and **le/Le** means *she/it/you* formal, *her/it* fem./*you* formal, and *to her*/to it/*to you* formal. Use the upper case **L** to indicate the *you* formal for the personal, direct, and indirect object pronouns. This isn't always the case, but it's a useful tool for distinguishing between the two options.

These days, **gli** *(to them)* is more frequently used to replace **loro**, to mean *to them*. But **gli** can also mean *to him*, so here is another example when context matters.

Chapter **3**

Expressing Yourself in the Present

N avigating the present tense is an important step toward proficiency in Italian because in many cases it's all you need for basic communicative needs. The present tense is super useful for most people, because that's where the action and interest is — in the here and now. In Italian, the overwhelming majority of present-tense verbs are regular and predictable, very simple to use, and follow dependable conjugations. However, some verbs are irregular and walk to the beat of a different drummer; for these verbs, you have to memorize their patterns or conjugations.

In this chapter, I introduce you to Italian verbs in their infinitive form, make you comfortable with the personal pronouns, and then take a deep dive into the present tense of regular, irregular, and reflexive verbs. The present tense takes two forms in Italian:

» **Present tense:** Also called the *present indicative*.

» **Present progressive tense:** Facilitates talking about what's happening or what you're doing only at a specific moment.

Getting to Know Italian Verbs

In Italian, just like in English, every verb has an **infinito** *(infinitive)* form — the form of the verb you'd find if you looked it up in the dictionary. English often couples infinitives with the word *to,* as in *to eat* or *to drink.*

TIP

Infinitives are amazing bridges when learning Italian. Many nouns and adjectives are derived from verbs, so when you learn a verb, you often learn a noun and an adjective at the same time.

REMEMBER

All infinitives in Italian fall under three main verb types, also known as *conjugations.* I usually just call them **-are, -ere,** and **-ire** verbs:

>> **-are verbs:** Known as *first conjugation verbs,* such as **parlare** *(to speak)*

>> **-ere verbs:** Known as *second conjugation verbs,* such as **prendere** *(to take, to have)*

>> **-ire verbs:** Known as *third conjugation verbs,* such as **partire** *(to depart)* and **capire** *(to understand)*

Each infinitive verb also has its own stem (or *root*). The *stem* of the infinitive is what you have left after you take the **-are, -ere,** or **-ire** ending off of it. For example:

>> With **-are** verbs like **parlare** *(to speak),* the stem is **parl-.**

>> With **-ere** verbs like **prendere** *(to take, to have),* the stem is **prend-.**

>> With **-ire** verbs like **capire** *(to understand),* the stem is **cap-.**

Most stems follow this pattern and are regular. Stems are essential because they're the structures to which you attach the different verb endings of the different tenses. And most tenses use these stems (with the exception of the future and conditional tenses, which I discuss in Chapters 7 and 8).

Getting Personal with the Subject Pronouns

Chapter 1 introduces the *subject pronouns* (also known as *personal pronouns*), but here I provide more detail about them. The personal pronouns are an immediate indicator of the subject of the sentence. Table 3-1 provides you with a breakdown of the three persons in both their singular and plural forms.

TABLE 3-1 Subject Pronouns

Person	Singular	Meaning	Plural	Meaning
First	io	*I*	noi	*we*
Second	tu	*you,* informal	voi	*you (all)*
Third	lui, lei	*he, she, it*	loro	*they*
Third (Used to address people formally)	Lei	*you,* formal	Loro	*you,* formal

TIP

Lei can mean both *she* and the *you* formal, sing. Context will help you to determine between the two.

For Italian language learners, it's a common convention to help distinguish between the uppercase **Lei** (*you* formal) and the lowercase **lei** (*she*). When you're beginning a sentence, the **lei** (she) becomes **Lei** (she), of course. The same distinction marks the difference between **Loro** (*you* formal plural) and **loro** (*they*).

REMEMBER

Verbs need to agree with their pronouns. So, whenever I say *first person singular,* I mean the **io** (*I*) person and the first person singular of the verb; when I say the first person plural, I mean the **noi** (*we*) person of both the pronoun and the verb, and so forth.

Being inclusive

Another important point: In certain areas of the United States, especially in inclusive schools and universities, people more frequently express their preferred pronoun according to the gender with which they identify *(she, her, hers; he, his, his; they, their, theirs).* Although this practice isn't as common in Italy yet as in the United States, some schools have launched something called *carriera ALIAS,* which encourages students and faculty to declare their pronoun preference by choosing between **lui** and **lei** (but not **loro**).

When my students choose *they, their, theirs* as pronouns, I ask them to choose between masculine and feminine endings in the Italian classroom because otherwise verb and adjective agreement just doesn't work. When writing, many Italianists in the United States use the asterisk * or the *schwa (ə)*, which is an effective way to get around privileging one gender over the other.

For example, **Car* student*** *(Dear students)* and **Carə colleghə** *(Dear colleagues)* could be a way to avoid defaulting to the conventional masculine ending when addressing your students or colleagues.

Knowing when to use them

Even though you definitely have to know how the personal pronouns work, most of the time, you don't always need personal pronouns in Italian because the verb conjugations indicate the subject. In the sentence **Guardano la televisione tutte le sere** *(They watch TV every night)*, you know the subject is **loro** *(they)* because **guardano** *(they watch, they're watching)* is conjugated in the third-person plural form (and the *they* meaning is included in the verb itself).

REMEMBER

At times, though, you do need subject pronouns. You should use them whenever you're emphasizing what a particular person is doing:

> **Io andrò alle Cinque Terre, non Antonietta.** *(I'm going to the Cinque Terre, not Antonietta.)*

Knowing when to use tu versus Lei

You can address people either formally or informally in Italian, altering your pronoun and verb choice accordingly. I discuss which pronouns to use under certain circumstances here.

Being informal

Use the informal **tu** and **voi** only with friends, family, children, relatives, teenagers, and with people your age (until you hit adulthood).

Generally, when you use someone's first name, you use the **tu**. Informally, you address people with the following pronoun-verb combinations:

» **tu** (*you* singular) + the verb in the second-person singular

[Tu] vieni alla partita, Andrea? *(Are you coming to the game, Andrea?)*

» **voi** (*you* plural) + the verb in the second-person plural

[Voi] venite alla partita, Andrea e Giacomo? *(Are you coming to the game, Andrea and Giacomo?)*

Going formal

Use the formal **Lei** when addressing those whom you don't know well, elders, professors, servers, salespeople, your friends' parents, and so forth.

You want to be respectful, so always use the formal when in doubt! Formally, you address people with the following pronoun-verb combinations:

» **Lei** *(you)*: With adults (or anyone you need to be formal with) + the verb in the third-person singular:

[Lei] viene alla partita, Signore/Signora? *(Are you coming to the game, Sir/Ma'am?)*

» Nowadays, on the other hand, you can use **voi** to address more than one person either informally or formally:

[Voi] venite alla partita? *(Are you all coming to the game?)*

The formal plural **Loro** is rarely used these days.

Diving deeper: Formal or informal

When you address someone formally, you can use their last name preceded by their title — **Signor** (*Mr.*), **Signora** (*Mrs.*, *Ms.*), **Signorina** (*Miss*, *Ms.*), **Dottor/Dottoressa** (*Dr.*, for all those with a university degree), **Professor/Professoressa/Prof.**, and so on. If you're uncertain what gender to use when addressing someone, side with caution and simply use the third person of the verb, without any title. For example: the question **Gradisce ancora del vino**? (*Would you like more wine?*), employs the third person formal

Lei of the verb, without using a title. One exception where you could use a title even while being cautious about gender is with the abbreviation **Prof.** *(Professor)*, which can be gender neutral.

TIP

The comma that appears after someone's name or a term is a dead giveaway that you're dealing with a direct address and that you need **tu, voi,** or **Lei** — and the corresponding verb ending — according to context.

For example, compare how Beppe is being spoken to and spoken about in the following sentences:

> **Beppe, (tu) vieni al concerto?** *(Beppe, are you coming to the concert?)*

> **Beppe viene al concerto.** *(Beppe is coming to the concert.)*

Tu requires the verb form of the second person singular — for example, **tu sei** *(you are)*. **Lei** calls for the third person singular **Lei è** *(you are* [formal sing.]).

In Italian, unlike some other Romance languages, current usage still dictates the use of the formal singular **Lei** where appropriate. The plural *you* formal **Loro** has gone by the wayside, for the most part. One way to address a group of people a little more formally is to avoid the informal **ciao** in lieu of the more formal **Buongiorno.**

Exploring the Present Tense

The present tense allows you to talk about the present (obviously!), such as **oggi** *(today)* or **stasera** *(this evening)*, and sometimes about the future (not so obviously), such as **domani** *(tomorrow)*. The present tense takes two forms in Italian:

>> **Present tense:** Also called the *present indicative,* this tense describes current situations, what's happening or what you're doing at a specific moment, recurring actions, and habits:

- **Noi viviamo in Italia.** *(We live in Italy.)*

- **Finisco i compiti e poi esco.** *(I'm going to finish my homework and then go out.)*

>> **Present progressive tense:** This term facilitates talking about what's happening or what you're doing only at a specific moment, by using a gerund, which translates in English as "*I am __ ing*":

- **Ciao Paola, cosa fai?** *(Hi Paola, what are you doing?)*

- **Sto camminando.** *(I'm walking.)*

Conjugating Regular Verbs

You conjugate verbs in the present tense by using a verb stem and an ending. The infinitive — such as *to work, to play, to read*, and so forth — is the default form of the verb. In Italian, almost all infinitives end in **-are, -ere,** or **-ire.** When you take these endings out, you're left with the stem of the verb. Then, you add the endings. The following shows the pattern for creating a stem, illustrated by three regular verbs.

Infinitive Ending	Example	Stem
-are	**guardare** *(to look at, to watch)*	**guard-**
-ere	**correre** *(to run)*	**corr-**
-ire	**sentire** *(to hear, to taste, to feel, to touch)*	**sent-**

TIP

To negate something, simply place the word **non** in front of the verb:

Balli bene? *(Do you dance well?)*

No, non ballo bene. (*No, I don't dance well.*) (The **no** is optional; the **non** is necessary.)

The following sections show you how to form the present indicative of regular verbs, simply by adding three sets of endings to the stems of the three different verb conjugations.

Focusing on -are verbs

After you determine your stem, to conjugate a verb you only have to apply the appropriate endings. The endings for -**are** verbs are -**o**, -**i**, -**a**, -**iamo**, -**ate**, and -**ano**.

The following table conjugates the present indicative of **guardare** (*to look at, to watch*). Drop the verb at its stem (**guard-**) and add the endings.

Conjugation	Translation
io guardo	*I watch/do watch/am watching*
tu guardi	*you watch/you do watch/are watching*
lui/lei/Lei guarda	*He/she/it watches/does watch/is watching/ You (formal) watch/do watch/are watching*
noi guardiamo	*We watch/do watch/are watching*
voi guardate	*Y'all watch/do watch/are watching*
loro/Loro guardano	*They watch/do watch/are watching*

TIP

When you ask a question and then answer it, the words *do* and *does* are inferred.

> **Guardate sempre la partita?** *(Do you always watch the game?)*

The English words *is* and *are* are also inferred in questions, as well as in declarative sentences.

> **Emilia mangia con voi stasera?** *(Is Emilia eating with you tonight?)*

Listing every possible -**are** verb here is impossible (at least, not without a lot more paper), so I include some of my favorites:

- **arrivare** *(to arrive)*
- **ballare** *(to dance)*
- **cenare** *(to have dinner)*
- **cercare** *(to look for)*
- **cominciare** *(to begin)*
- **cucinare** *(to cook)*

- **giocare** *(to play a sport, cards)*
- **guidare** *(to drive)*
- **imparare** *(to learn)*
- **lavorare** *(to work)*
- **mangiare** *(to eat)*

>> **nuotare** *(to swim)*

>> **pagare** *(to pay)*

>> **parlare** *(to talk, to speak)*

>> **studiare** *(to study)*

>> **suonare** *(to play an instrument)*

REMEMBER

Suonare means *to play* **uno strumento musicale** *(a musical instrument)*, such as **la batteria** *(the drums)*, **la chitarra** *(the guitar)*, **il pianoforte** *(the piano)*, and **il violino** *(the violin)*.

Giocare means *to play a game* (**una partita**), and *a sport* (**uno sport**), such as **il calcio** *(soccer)*, **la pallacanestro** *(basketball)*, **la pallavolo** *(volleyball)* and **il tennis** *(tennis)*. In Italian, however, to say you *play a sport*, add the preposition **a**: **giocare a calcio, a pallacanestro, a pallavolo, a tennis**:

> **Mi piace guardare il tennis, e gioco a pallavolo.** *(I like to watch tennis, and I play volleyball.)*

See the Appendix for a few spelling/pronunciation variations that occur with verbs ending in **-care, -gare, -ciare**, and **-giare**, such as **giocare** *(to play)*, **pagare** *(to pay)*, **cominciare** *(to begin)*, **mangiare** *(to eat)*, **and studiare** *(to study)*.

Concentrating on -ere verbs

The following delineates the endings for the verbs of the second conjugation, **-ere** verbs, which are **-o, -i. -e, -iamo, -ete,** and **-ono**.

The following table conjugates the present indicative of **vedere** *(to see)*. Drop the verb at its stem **ved-**, and add the **ere** verb endings.

Conjugation	Translation
io vedo	*I see/do see/am seeing*
tu vedi	*you see/do see/are seeing*
lui/lei/Lei vede	*he/she/it sees/does see/is seeing/you (formal) see/do see/are seeing*
noi vediamo	*we see/do see/are seeing*
voi vedete	*y'all see/do see/are seeing*
loro/ Loro vedono	*they see/do see/are seeing*

Any present tense verb can sound like a gerund, depending on the context, such as in the following example:

Vediamo Margherita sabato. *(We're seeing Margherita on Saturday.)*

Here are some common **-ere** verbs:

>> **cadere** *(to fall)*

>> **chiedere** *(to ask for)*

>> **chiudere** *(to close)*

>> **convincere** *(to convince)*

>> **conoscere** *(to know)*

>> **correre** *(to run)*

>> **leggere** *(to read)*

>> **mettere** *(to put/ to place)*

>> **perdere** *(to lose)*

>> **prendere** *(to take; to have* [as in what you're having in a restaurant or bar])

>> **ripetere** *(to repeat)*

>> **rispondere** *(to answer)*

>> **scrivere** *(to write)*

>> **vedere** *(to see)*

>> **vincere** *(to win)*

REMEMBER

The verb **bere** (*to drink*) is an exception to the standard **-ere** conjugation rules only because you have to alter the stem first, from **ber-** to **bev-**, and then add the **-ere** endings.

bere *(to drink)*

io bevo	**noi beviamo**
tu bevi	**voi bevete**
lui/lei/Lei beve	**loro/Loro bevono**

Bevono solo acqua. *(They drink only water.)*

Eyeing -ire verbs

Italian has two types of **-ire** verbs:

>> **-ire verbs:** The first kind follows a regular pattern without undergoing any change.

>> **-ire/isc:** The second type, what you can call the **-ire/isc** verbs, follows the exact same pattern, but you need to throw

in an **-isc-** between the stem and the **-ire** endings, in all the persons except for **noi** and **voi**.

Table 3-2 outlines the differences between an **–ire** verb and an **–ire/isc** verb. Create the stem first, and then add on the endings (**aprire** *[to open]* becomes **apr-** and **capire** *[to understand]* becomes **cap-**). Note that the endings (the last letters) are exactly the same in both types. Make a conscious note as well of how the **–ire** endings compare to the **–ere** and the **–are** endings.

The pronunciation of the **c** sound in the **–ire/isc** verbs is odd in that it's both hard, like in **capisco/capiscono** (with a *k* sound) and soft, like in **capisci/capisce** (with a *sh* sound).

Students of Italian frequently wonder how to tell the difference between **–ire** verbs and **–ire/isc** verbs. Work to remember the **–ire/isc** verbs presented in this section, and then add on when you encounter more.

Here are some common **–ire** verbs:

>> **aprire** *(to open)*

>> **dormire** *(to sleep)*

>> **partire** *(to leave/to depart)*

>> **sentire** *(to hear/to taste/to smell/to touch)*

Here are some common **–ire/isc** verbs:

>> **capire** *(to understand)*

>> **finire** *(to finish)*

>> **preferire** *(to prefer)*

>> **pulire** *(to clean)*

Preferire *(to prefer)* is a special verb in that you can follow it with a noun and a verb. Here are examples of both:

Preferisci il pesce o la carne stasera? *(Do you prefer fish or meat this evening?)*

You can also follow **preferire** with an infinitive:

> **Mio padre preferisce restare a casa.** *(My father prefers to stay home.)*

TABLE 3-2 **Present Tense Endings of -ire Verbs**

-ire Verb	Meaning	-ire/isc Verb	Meaning
io apro	*I open/do open/I'm opening*	**io capisco**	*I understand/do understand/am understanding*
tu apri	*You open/You're opening*	**tu capisci**	*You understand/do understand/are understanding*
lui/lei/Lei apre	*He/she/it opens/does open/is opening; you (formal) open/do open/are opening*	**lui/lei/Lei capisce**	*He/she/it understands/does understand/is understanding; you (formal) understand/do understand/are understanding*
noi apriamo	*We open/do open/are opening*	**noi capiamo**	*We understand/do understand/are understanding*
voi aprite	*You all open/do open/are opening*	**voi capite**	*You all understand/do understand/are understanding*
loro/Loro aprono	*They open/do open/are opening*	**loro/Loro capiscono**	*They understand/do understand/are understanding*
	You (plural formal) open/do open/are opening		*You (plural formal) understand/do understand/are understanding*

Identifying similarities with the three verb types

The three verb types (**-are, -ere,** and **-ire**) have a couple of commonalities.

The **noi** ending is always the same, no matter the verbs' endings: **iamo.**

REMEMBER

The **voi** ending always takes the vowel that's characteristic of the verb type, which I illustrate by underlining the third to the last letter of the following three verbs:

>> **Mangiare** = **mangiate** *(You all eat./You all do eat./You all are eating.)*

>> **Ricevere** = **ricevete** *(You all receive./You all do receive./You all are receiving.)*

>> **Partire** = **partite** *(You all leave/depart./You all do leave/depart./You all are leaving/departing.)*

Tackling Irregular Verbs

What fun would Italian be if you didn't have to tackle some irregular verbs? Now I introduce you to a slew of irregular verbs, most of which you use in your daily comings and goings.

Here, I show you how to form the present tense of many irregular Italian verbs, including the two most important verbs, **essere** *(to be)* and **avere** *(to have)*. Although some of them follow reliable patterns, which I share with you, others play by their own rules.

Looking at irregular -are verbs

Andare *(to go)*, **dare** *(to give)*, **fare** *(to do/to make)*, and **stare** *(to stay/to be)* are the only irregular verbs of this conjugation, but they're quite important and very versatile. *Note:* These verbs have some similarities, such as the **i** in the **tu** person and the double **nn** in the **loro** person. Grouping these verbs together can help you remember their commonalities. Throughout this chapter, I put an asterisk near the regular forms to emphasize them.

andare *(to go)*

io vado	noi andiamo*
tu vai	voi andate*
lui/lei/Lei va	loro/Loro vanno

Andiamo sempre nello stesso ristorante.
(We always go to the same restaurant.)

dare *(to give)*

io do*	noi diamo*
tu dai	voi date*
lui/lei/Lei dà (always accented)	loro/Loro danno

Dà un libro alla vicina. *(He/she is giving the neighbor a book.)*

fare *(to do, to make)*

io faccio	noi facciamo
tu fai	voi fate*
lui/lei/Lei fa*	loro/Loro fanno

Faccio una torta. *(I'm making a cake.)*

stare *(to stay/to be)*

io sto*	noi stiamo*
tu stai	voi state*
lui/lei/Lei sta*	loro/Loro stanno

Stiamo bene. *(We're well.)*

Italian has idiomatic uses (exceptions in meaning) as well as set meanings to these verbs that don't translate word for word into English. Here are several; some are intuitive (and others mean what they say):

>> **andare d'accordo** *(to get along)*

>> **andare al cinema** *(to go to the movies)*

>> **andare in vacanza** *(to go on vacation)*

>> **andare in macchina, in treno, in autobus, in aereo** *(to go by car, by train, by bus, by plane)*

>> **andare a cavallo, a piedi** *(to go by horse, on foot)*

- >> **dare una mano** *(to give a hand/to help)*
- >> **dare un esame** *(to take a test)*
- >> **dare fastidio** *(to bother)*
- >> **dare da mangiare** *(to feed)*
- >> **stare zittto** *(to be quiet)*
- >> **stare attetonto** *(to pay attention)*
- >> **stare bene/male** *(to be well/to be not well)*
- >> **fare una domanda** *(to ask a question)*
- >> **fare caldo, fare freddo** *(to be hot/to be cold* as in, inside or outside; impersonal verb that uses only the third-person singular)
- >> **fare colazione** *(to have breakfast)*
- >> **fare una passeggiata** *(to take a walk)*
- >> **fare una gita** *(to take an excursion/to take a day trip)*
- >> **fare una foto** *(to take a picture)*
- >> **non fa niente** *(it doesn't matter)*

When you talk about the weather, you use the third person of the verb, such as:

Che tempo fa? *(What's the weather like?)*

Fa caldo! *(It's hot!)*

Fa bello! *(It's nice out!)*

Piove! *(It's raining!)*

Exploring the modal auxiliaries

Most irregular verbs are **-ere** verbs, so it's impossible to list them all here. I walk you through some of the most commonly used ones.

Modal verbs, which provide different nuances to what you're saying, also act as auxiliaries; they're frequently followed by the infinitive of the main verb.

It sounds just as impolite to say **Voglio un gelato** *(I want an ice cream)* in Italian as it does in English. So, keep in mind that you should use the conditional tense (see Chapter 8) **vorrei** *(I would like)*, when you want to be polite.

The following tables show conjugations of each of the modal auxiliary verbs. Notice that for some of the persons, **dovere** takes the stem **dev-** + the **-ere** endings.

dovere *(must/to have to/to need to/ought to)*

io devo	noi dobbiamo
tu devi	voi dovete*
lui/lei/Lei deve	loro/Loro devono

Devono andare a casa. *(They have to go home.)*

potere *(can/may)*

io posso	noi possiamo
tu puoi	voi potete*
lui/lei/Lei può	loro/Loro possono

Può giocare con noi. *(He/she can play with us.)*

volere *(to want)*

io voglio	noi vogliamo
tu vuoi	voi volete*
lui/lei/Lei vuole	loro/Loro vogliono

Vogliono vederti. *(They want to see you.)*

Differentiating between sapere and conoscere

Both the verbs **sapere** and **conoscere** mean *to know* in Italian, whereas English uses only one verb. **Sapere** is irregular, and **conoscere** is regular — but if you study them side by side, you can more easily keep their meaning and usage separate. Use the following rules to help you identify when to use each:

>> **Sapere** can generally be followed by a verb in the infinitive or an *interrogative* word — meaning a word that you use to ask a question (see Chapter 5 for more on interrogatives):

>> **Conoscere** means *to know* someone or something, as in to be acquainted with:

Taking on irregular -ire verbs

The -**ire** verbs have fewer irregular verbs, which follow some basic patterns. The most frequent and essential -**ire** verbs are **dire** *(to say)*, **venire** *(to come)*, and **uscire** *(to go out)*. Commit this set of verbs to memory by using whatever strategy works for you.

Conjugating dire

Notice that the verb **dire** *(to say/to tell)* takes **dic-** as its stem in some persons, but the endings are the regular -**ire** endings:

dire *(to say/to tell)*	
io dico	noi diciamo
tu dici	voi dite*
lui/lei/Lei dice	loro/Loro dicono

Maria e Lee dicono che comprano una casa nuova.
(Maria and Lee say they're buying a new house.)

Be careful with your pronunciation of the **c** in **dire, dico,** and **dicono** have a *k* sound, but **dici, dice,** and **diciamo** have a *ch* sound.

REMEMBER

Conjugating venire

The verb **venire** *(to come)* undergoes a slight stem change in some persons and also adds a **g** in others, while keeping two regular persons + the regular -**ire** endings. Even though it's all over the place, it follows a pattern.

venire *(to come)*	
io vengo	noi veniamo*
tu vieni	voi venite*
lui/lei/Lei viene	loro/Loro vengono

Veniamo a Livorno il diciotto giugno.
(We're coming to Livorno on June eighteenth.)

Conjugating uscire

The verb **uscire** takes **esc-** as its stem for its irregular persons and then keeps the regular **-ire** endings for all of its persons. The **c** in **esco** and **escono** have a hard *c* (*k*) sound, and the **c** in **esci**, **esce**, **usciamo**, and **uscite** has a *sh* sound. Practice reading this verb aloud:

uscire *(to go out)*

io esco	noi usciamo*
tu esci	voi uscite*
lui/lei/Lei esce	loro/Loro escono

Marcella esce spesso con Tram. *(Marcella goes out often with Tram.)*

Working with essere and avere

Two of the most common verbs in the Italian language are irregular — **essere** *(to be)* and **avere** *(to have)*. Understanding the meaning and the usage of these two verbs is fundamental to learning Italian. I explore each in the following sections.

Using essere

The verb **essere** in the present tense in Italian essentially has the same function as *to be* does in English:

Essere o non essere. *(To be or not to be.)*

The following shows the conjugation of the verb **essere**:

essere *(to be)*

io sono	noi siamo
tu sei	voi siete
lui/lei/Lei è	loro/Loro sono

Sono stanca. *(I'm tired.)*

ESSERE WITH ADJECTIVES

You can use **essere** with adjectives, just like you can with *to be* in English — with one caveat: Most adjectives must agree in gender or in gender and number with the noun (depending on the adjective). See Chapter 4 for more on adjective agreement. See the following:

> **Gaby, sei italiana?** *(Gaby, are you Italian?)*
>
> **No, Teresa, non sono italiana, sono uruguiana.** *(No, Teresa, I am not Italian, I am Uruguayan.)*

When you wish to negate something in the simplest way, just add **non** *(not)* in front of the verb.

REMEMBER

ESSERE WITH CI

By itself, **ci** sometimes means *there*. You can combine it with **essere** to mean *there is* and *there are*, and to also ask the questions *is there?* and *are there?* Use **c'è** for *there is/is there*:

> Phone rings: **Pronto, c'è Serena?** *(Hello, is Serena there?)/* **No, non c'è.** *(No, she's not.)*

Use **ci sono** for *there are/are there*:

> **Ci sono venti regioni in Italia.** *(There are twenty regions in Italy.)*

Using avere

Knowing how to use the verb **avere** *(to have)* is an important marker of proficiency. The following table shows the conjugation of the verb **avere** *(to have)*.

The **h** is *always* silent in Italian: Just pretend it isn't there when you're speaking (and reading)!

REMEMBER

avere *(to have)*	
io ho	**noi abbiamo**
tu hai	**voi avete***
lui/lei/Lei ha	**loro/Loro hanno**

> **Quel ristorante ha dell'ottimo cibo.** *(That restaurant has great food.)*
>
> **Hanno una casa a Pescara.** *(They have a house in Pescara.)*

Avere has several idiomatic uses that need to be tucked away in your memory bank. Many, though not all, translate directly into English with the verb *to be*. For example, **Quanti anni hai?** *(How old are you?)* uses the verb **avere** rather than **essere.**

All of the terms following the verb **avere** in Table 3-3 are nouns, which explains why you use the verb **avere** rather than **essere.** So, you're literally saying *I have hunger* when you say **Ho fame.**

This table lists the most common idiomatic expressions that use **avere,** but they don't mean *to have.*

TABLE 3-3 **Idiomatic Expressions That Use Avere**

Expression	Example	Translation
avere . . . anni *(to be . . . years old)*	**Il mio cane ha dodici anni.**	*My dog is 12 years old.* (Literally: *My dog has 12 years.*)
avere bisogno di *(to need)*	**Ho bisogno di dormire.**	*I need to sleep.*
avere fame *(to be hungry)*	**Fatima ha fame.**	*Fatima is hungry.*
avere sete *(to be thirsty)*	**Matteo, hai sete?**	*Matteo, are you thirsty?*
avere caldo *(to be hot)*	**Abbiamo caldo!**	*We're hot!*
avere freddo *(to be cold)*	**Avete freddo?**	*Are you (all) cold?*
avere voglia di *(to feel like)*	**Ho voglia di un gelato.**	*I feel like having an ice-cream.*
avere sonno *(to be sleepy)*	**Ho sonno spesso a quest'ora.**	*I'm usually sleepy at this time.*

The infinitive of the verb follows the preposition **di** when used with expressions such as **avere voglia di** and **avere bisogno di,** depending on context. For example:

> **Chi ha voglia di giocare a bocce?** *(Who feels like playing bocce?)*

Using Reflexive Verbs

A *reflexive verb* is usually used when the subject of a sentence performs an action on itself. When translating Italian reflexive verbs into English, you can frequently — but not always! — throw in (or imagine) the words *myself, yourself,* and so on. In order to tell if a verb is a reflexive verb, look for the ending on the infinitive form: If the **-si** is attached, it's reflexive. Look at this short conversation:

Come ti chiami? *(What's your name?)*

Mi chiamo Teresa. *(My name is Teresa.)*

You use reflexive verbs in everyday life, all the time, to talk about your daily routine and how you feel:

Non mi sento bene. *(I don't feel well.)*

Mia figlia si veste in cinque minuti. *(My daughter gets dressed in five minutes.)*

These sections walk you through when to use reflexive verbs, introduce you to reflexive pronouns, and illustrate how to conjugate reflexive verbs in the present.

Knowing when to use reflexive verbs

You use reflexive verbs when

>> The subject is the object of its own action. This construct frequently suggests doing something to oneself.

   Mi lavo il viso. *(I'm washing my face.)* Note that this sentence doesn't use the Italian possessive adjective **mio** *(my).*

>> You're expressing a rich range of other moments that don't necessarily imply an action reflected back to the self, such as with the verb **dimenticarsi** *(to forget)*:

   Mi dimentico sempre le chiavi! *(I always forget my keys!)*

>> More than one person is involved (thus making it a reciprocal action), **such as the verb guardarsi** *(to look at each other).*

For this reason, reciprocals are always in the three plural persons **(noi, voi, loro)**:

- **ci guardiamo** *(we look at each other/we're looking at each other)*

- **vi guardate** *(you look at each other/you're looking at each other)*

- **si guardano** *(they look at each other/they're looking at each other)*

Looking at reflexive pronouns

Reflexive pronouns convey that the subject is also frequently the recipient of the action:

Il mio gatto si lava sempre. *(My cat always washes/cleans himself.)*

You use reflexive pronouns with reflexive verbs. Table 3-4 presents the reflexive pronouns.

TABLE 3-4 Reflexive Pronouns

Singular	Plural
mi *(myself)*	**ci** *(ourselves)*
ti *(yourself)*	**vi** *(yourselves, informal)*
si *(himself/herself/itself)*	**si** *(themselves)*
Si *(yourself,* third-person sing., formal)	**Si** *(yourselves,* third-person pl., formal)

The uppercase **S** of the third person singular and plural **Si** indicates formal address. This helps distinguish the lowercase **si** *(himself/herself/itself)* from the upper case formal *yourself/yourselves.*

Forming reflexive verbs

One of the tricks to conjugating a reflexive verb in the present (or any other tense) is to remember this format:

Reflexive pronoun + Conjugated verb (without the **-si** attached)

To conjugate a reflexive verb, just follow these steps (I use the verb **lavarsi** *[to wash oneself/to get washed/to bathe]* as an example):

1. **Remove the final vowel and the** si **from** lavarsi.

You're left with the infinitive, in this case.

lavare, a regular **-are** verb

2. **Remove the -are ending.**

You're left with the stem **lav-**.

3. **Conjugate the infinitive verb by adding the appropriate present tense endings.**

The **-are** endings are **-o, i, a, iamo, ate, ano.**

Annamaria si lava spesso il viso. *(Annamaria washes her face often.)*

4. **Place the appropriate reflexive pronoun before the verb:**

Francesca, ti lavi le mani prima di cena? *(Francesca, are you going to wash your hands before dinner?)*

The following tables show you four regular reflexive verbs conjugated in the present: an –**are**, –**ere**, –**ire**, and –**ire (isc)** verb.

You don't need the personal pronouns (**io, tu, lui/lei/Lei, noi, voi, loro**) when conjugating the reflexive verbs; they're even redundant at times. I include the personal pronouns in the **lavarsi** table only to remind you what they are. You *do* always need the reflexive pronouns in these conjugations, though.

lavarsi *(to wash oneself)*

io mi lavo	**noi ci laviamo**
tu ti lavi	**voi vi lavate**
lui/lei/Lei si lava	**loro/Loro si lavano**

Ci laviamo le mani prima di mangiare. *(We wash our hands before eating.)*

mettersi *(to put something on/to wear something)*

mi metto	ci mettiamo
ti metti	vi mettete
si mette	si mettono

Mi metto le scarpe da ginnastica. *(I'm putting on my sneakers.)*

divertirsi *(to have fun/to enjoy oneself/to have a good time)*

mi diverto	ci divertiamo
ti diverti	vi divertite
si diverte	si divertono

Ci divertiamo stasera! *(We're going to have fun this evening!)*

trasferirsi *(to move [to a place])*

mi trasferisco	ci trasferiamo
ti trasferisci	vi trasferite
si trasferisce	si trasferiscono

Giancarlo si trasferisce a Ravenna quando va in pensione.
(Giancarlo is going to move to Ravenna when he retires.)

Table 3-5 lists some common reflexive verbs. Pick out the ones that you find most useful.

TABLE 3-5 Common Reflexive Verbs

Verb	Meaning	Verb	Meaning
addormentarsi	*to fall asleep*	offendersi	*to get/be offended*
alzarsi	*to get up, to stand up*	ricordarsi	*to remember*
annoiarsi	*to get bored*	rilassarsi	*to relax*
arrabbiarsi	*to get angry*	scusarsi	*to apologize*
chiamarsi	*to be called*	sedersi	*to sit*
curarsi	*to take care of oneself*	sentirsi	*to feel*

Verb	Meaning	Verb	Meaning
dimenticarsi	*to forget*	spogliarsi	*to get undressed*
divertirsi	*to enjoy oneself/ to have fun*	sposarsi [con]	*to get married*
farsi male	*to get hurt*	stancarsi	*to get tired*
fermarsi	*to stop*	svegliarsi	*to wake up*
fidanzarsi	*to get engaged*	svestirsi	*to undress*
innamorarsi	*to fall in love*	tagliarsi	*to cut oneself*
lamentarsi	*to complain*	vestirsi	*to get dressed*

TIP

A note about **innamorarsi** *(to fall in love)*: This verb can be both reflexive and reciprocal. **Innamorarsi** is reflexive when you say **Mi innamoro facilmente** *(I fall in love easily)*, and it's reciprocal when you say **Ci siamo innamorati** *(We fell in love with each other).*

Liking piacere

The frequently used verb **piacere** *(to like; literally, to be pleasing to)* needs to be addressed separately.

You probably want to say **mi piace** *(I like)* or **non mi piace** *(I do not like)* practically every day, maybe even multiple times a day, so you need to be equipped to express your likes and dislikes easily and promptly in Italian.

Throughout this book, I talk about only two persons of **piacere: piace** and **piacciono** (third person singular and third person plural), because they are the easiest to use! **Piacere** uses indirect object pronouns instead of subject pronouns.

The following list breaks down the basics of these two:

>> **piace** (third-person singular): Use if what you like (or what anyone else likes) is singular or an infinitive:

Mi piace la pizza. Ti, gli/le, ci, vi, gli piace la pizza. *(I like pizza. You, he/she, we, you all, they like pizza.)* **Pizza** is singular.

Mi piace dormire. Ti, gli/le, ci, vi, gli. *(I like to sleep. You, he/she, we, you all, they like to sleep.)* **Dormire** is an infinitive.

>> **piacciono** (third-person plural): Use this if what you like is plural.

> **Mi piacciono le lasagne. Ti, gli/le, ci, vi, gli piacciono le lasagne.** *(I like lasagna. You, he/she, we, you all, they like lasagna.)* **Lasagne** is plural.

Check out these examples for additional usage:

> **Ti piace Urbino?** *(Do you like Urbino?)*
>
> **Sì, mi piace.** *(Yes, I do.)*
>
> **No, non mi piace.** *(No, I don't./No, I don't like it.)*

Note that the *do* and the *it* are implied.

Doing Things in the Here and Now — Present Progressive Tense

In Italian, you can convey that you're in the middle of doing something by using the present progressive tense. For instance, if someone asks you **Che cosa stai facendo?** *(What are you doing?)*, you can answer **Sto lavando la macchina** *(I'm washing the car)*. Use the present progressive when you want to emphasize what's happening in that specific moment:

> **Chiudi la finestra. Non vedi che sta piovendo?** *(Close the window. Don't you see it's raining?)*
>
> **Sta cominciando a piovere.** *(It's beginning to rain.)*

You form the present progressive tense by adding the gerund to the present tense of the verb **stare** *(to be)*, as in **Stiamo mangiando** *(We're eating)*. The gerund is invariable in gender and number, so you don't have to make it agree with any other word. To form it, you add -**ando** to the stem of an -**are** verb, or add -**endo** to the stem of an -**ere** or -**ire** verb. Easy peasy.

See how **stare** is conjugated in the "Looking at irregular -are verbs" section earlier in this chapter.

Table 3-6 shows how to create gerunds.

TABLE 3-6 **Creating Gerunds**

Verb Type	Infinitive	Gerund Ending	Gerund
-are	**guardare** *(to look at/ to watch)*	-ando	**guardando** *(looking)*
-ere	**leggere** *(to read)*	-endo	**leggendo** *(reading)*
-ire	**sentire** *(to hear/ to taste/to smell/to feel)*	-endo	**sentendo** *(hearing/ tasting)*
	finire *(to finish)*		**finendo** *(finishing)*

Most verbs form the gerund regularly. Even the **-ire/isc** verbs, which add **-isc-** to some persons, follow a regular pattern, such as **finendo** *(finishing)*.

REMEMBER

You have to deal with some irregular gerund forms when writing and speaking in Italian. Verbs that have irregular stems in the imperfect tense — such as **bere** *(to drink)*, **dire** *(to say, to tell)*, **fare** *(to do, to make)*, and so on — also have irregular stems when forming a gerund. However, after you isolate the irregular stem, you simply add the gerund ending:

The main irregular verbs appear in the following table.

Infinitive	Gerund
bere *(to drink)*	**bevendo** *(drinking)*
dire *(to say)*	**dicendo** *(saying)*
fare *(to do, to make)*	**facendo** *(doing)*

Here are two examples:

Sto dicendo la verità! *(I'm telling the truth!)*

La mamma sta facendo la spesa. *(Mom is grocery shopping.)*

Chapter **4**

Building Beautiful Sentences

This chapter is all about creating richer and more varied sentences. It explains how to make Italian adjectives agree with the words they refer to. It furthermore shows you how to use and form adverbs correctly. I also give you ways to compare and contrast people, places, and things with comparatives and superlatives. You also get a crash course on the greatest hits of Italian prepositions.

Making Adjectives Agree

In Italian, like in English, you employ adjectives to describe nouns, names, and pronouns. Most adjectives agree in number and gender with what they're describing, and then there are the ones that have a mind of their own.

If you say **Marcella ha una casa grande** (*Marcella has a big house*) or **Marcella ha una casa piccola** (*Marcella has a small house*), all you've changed is one word, but you've said two very different things. **Grande** (*big*) and **piccola** (*small*) are adjectives that convey qualities of people, animals, objects, and situations.

You need a masculine singular adjective to modify a masculine singular noun, a feminine singular adjective to modify a feminine singular noun, and so forth. For example, **Emilio è bello** (*Emilio is beautiful*) and **Emilia è bella** (*Emilia is beautiful*).

These sections show you two different kinds of regular adjectives, the ones that end in -**o** in their neutral form and the ones that end in -**e** in their neutral form. I spell out how to make both kinds of adjectives agree with nouns. You also get a dose of irregular adjectives.

Tackling regular adjectives

Regular adjectives modify only the last letter to change both gender and number (see Table 4-1) or only number (shown in Table 4-2).

TABLE 4-1 **Four-Ending Adjectives**

Ending	Gender and Number	Example Adjective	Example Phrase
-o	Masculine singular (m)	**italiano**	**il ragazzo italiano** *(the Italian boy)*
-a	Feminine singular (f)	**italiana**	**la ragazza italiana** *(the Italian girl)*
-i	Masculine plural (m/pl.)	**italiani**	**i ragazzi italiani** *(the Italian boys)*
-e	Feminine plural (f/pl.)	**italiane**	**le ragazze italiane** *(the Italian girls)*

TABLE 4-2 **Two-Ending Adjectives**

Ending	Number	Example Adjective	Example Phrase
-e	Singular (m., f.)	**intelligente**	**il cane intelligente** (m/sing.) *(the smart dog)* **la madre intelligente** (f/sing.) *(the smart mother)*
-i	Plural (m., f.)	**intelligenti**	**i cani intelligenti** (m/pl.) *(the smart dogs)* **le madri intelligenti** (f/pl.) *(the smart mothers)*

Note that the nouns I use in the examples in Table 4-2 — **cane** (m) and **madre** (f) — end in an -**e** but have their specific gender. (See Chapter 2 for the details on this type of noun that ends in -**e**.) Here are a couple more examples of some very common adjectives with four endings:

Chi è la tua attrice preferita? *(Who is your favorite actress?)*

Questi gnocchi sono deliziosi! *(These gnocchi are delicious!)*

Table 4-3 shows common adjectives that end in -**o** and -**e**. Although this list isn't exhaustive, if you understand how to make these adjectives agree, you'll know what to do with the other ones you encounter. I note which adjectives are *invariable* — they remain the same whether singular or plural.

TABLE 4-3 Common Adjectives (Color and Origin)

Colors	Nationalities	Italian Provenances (Regions/Cities)
arancione *(orange)*	**albanese** *(Albanian)*	**abruzzese** *(from Abruzzi)*
azzurro *(light blue)*	**americano** *(American)*	**bolognese** *(from Bologna)*
bianco *(white)*	**australiano** *(Australian)*	**genovese** *(from Genoa)*
blu *(dark blue,* inv.)	**cinese** *(Chinese)*	**lombardo** *(from Lombardy)*
grigio *(gray)*	**greco** *(Greek)*	**marchigiano** *(from the Marche)*
marrone *(brown)*	**indiano** *(Indian)*	**milanese** *(from Milano)*
nero *(black)*	**italiano** *(Italian)*	**napoletano** *(from Naples)*
rosa (*pink,* inv.)	**messicano** *(Mexican)*	**pugliese** *(from Puglia)*
rosso *(red)*	**rumeno** *(Romanian)*	**romano** *(Roman)*
verde *(green)*	**russo** *(Russian)*	**sardo** *(Sardinian)*
viola (*purple,* inv.)	**senegalese** *(Senegalese)*	**siciliano** *(Sicilian)*
	tedesco *(German)*	**veneto** *(from the Veneto region)*

One good way to remember adjectives is to categorize them with their opposite meaning, as shown in Table 4-4.

TABLE 4-4 Adjectives with Opposites

Adjective	Opposite
basso (*short*, as in stature)	**alto** *(tall)*
bello *(beautiful)*	**brutto** *(ugly)*
biondo *(blond)*	**bruno** *(brunette)*
buono *(good)*	**cattivo** *(bad/mean)*
carino *(cute)*	**brutto** *(ugly)*
comodo *(comfortable)*	**scomodo** *(uncomfortable)*
contento/felice *(happy)*	**triste** *(sad)*
corto (*short;* as in hair or a dress)	**lungo** *(long)*
costoso/caro *(expensive)*	**economico** *(cheap)*
divertente *(fun)*	**noioso** *(boring)*
facile *(easy)*	**difficile** *(difficult/hard)*
generoso *(generous)*	**avaro** *(stingy)*
gentile *(kind)*	**crudele** *(cruel/mean)*
grasso *(fat)*	**magro** *(thin)*
inclusivo *(inclusive)*	**esclusivo** *(exclusive)*
intelligente *(intelligent/smart)*	**stupido** *(stupid)*
interessante *(interesting)*	**noioso** *(boring)*
lento *(slow)*	**veloce** *(fast)*
onesto *(honest)*	**disonesto** *(dishonest)*
ricco *(rich)*	**povero** *(poor)*
simpatico *(nice)*	**antipatico** *(unpleasant)*
stesso *(same)*	**diverso** *(different)*
timido *(shy)*	**socievole** *(outgoing)*

Regular adjectives with a twist: bello and buono

Bello (*beautiful*) and **buono** (*good*) are common regular adjectives in Italian. When used after a noun, they're regular adjectives that have four possible endings (refer to Table 4-1). However, when used before a noun, they take on more forms, depending on the gender and number of the noun they modify. **Bello** works very much like the contracted prepositions I discuss in the section "Contracting prepositions with articles and nouns" later in this chapter.

Beginning	Singular	Plural
s- + consonant; or **z-**	**bello/bella**	**begli/belle**
other consonants	**bel/bella**	**bei/belle**
vowels	**bell'/bell'**	**begli/belle**

Note how **bello** differs in the following two sentences:

Che begli occhi che hai! *(What beautiful eyes you have!)*

Gli occhi di Emilia sono belli *(Emilia's eyes are beautiful.)*

Buono follows the rules of the indefinite article (see Chapter 2). Note the similarities in the following:

Indefinite Article	Buono
un amico	**buon amico**
un'amica	**buon'amica**
uno zoo	**buono zio**
una persona	**buona persona**

Note how **uno** and **buono** illustrate the previously mentioned similarity in the following two sentences:

Mariapaola è un'amica. *(Mariapaola is a friend.)*

Maripaola è una buon'amica. *(Mariapaola is a good friend.)*

Irregular adjectives

Some irregular adjectives undergo a spelling modification, usually to preserve the soft or hard sound of the singular masculine, as in **bianco, bianca, bianchi, bianche** (*white*); others have a special ending in –**ista**, which has only one singular form, regardless of gender. For example, **Gerardo è molto ottimista** (*Gerald is very optimistic*).

Table 4-5 breaks down the ending changes for irregular adjectives, with examples.

TABLE 4-5 Variations of Irregular Adjective Endings

Type of Adjective	Singular Ending Change	Plural Ending Change	Singular Examples	Plural Examples
-ista	-ista (m/f)	-isti (m); -iste (f)	ottimista (m/f)	ottimisti (m); ottimiste (f)
Two-syllable adjective	-co, -go, -ca, or -ga	-chi, -ghi, -che, or -ghe	bianco (m); bianca (f)	bianchi (m); bianche (f)
			lungo (m); lunga (f)	lunghi (m); lunghe (f)
Multi-syllable adjective	-co or -ca	-ci or -che	simpatico (m); simpatica (f)	simpatici (m); simpatiche (f)

Other adjectives ending in –**ista** include

>> **egoista** *(selfish)*

>> **pessimista** *(pessimistic)*

>> **socialista** *(socialist)*

Invariable adjectives

A few adjectives are invariable, meaning that the ending remains the same regardless of what the noun's gender or number is. Key invariable adjectives include the adjectives for color: **blu** (*blue*), **beige** (*beige*), **rosa** (*pink*), **viola** (*violet/purple*).

Putting adjectives in their place

WARNING

In English, as in Italian, you generally place adjectives after verbs, such as **Olivia è contenta** (*Olivia is happy*). More importantly however, when you match an adjective to a noun, in English you place it before the noun to which it refers, as in a *blue sky*. In Italian, you usually do the opposite, and the adjective comes *after* the noun, as in **cielo azzurro** (which translates as *blue sky*).

Here's a list of the most important adjectives that generally precede the noun:

>> **bello** *(beautiful)*

>> **brutto** *(ugly)*

>> **buono** *(good)*

>> **cattivo** *(nasty/evil)*

>> **breve** *(short)*

>> **lungo** *(long)*

For example: **Che bella giornata!** *(What a nice day!)*

Forming Adverbs the Italian Way

Adverbs are another important way of adding nuance to language. In Italian, adverbs are invariable, which means that you don't need to worry about making them agree with the words they modify. You can add an adverb to qualify a verb, an adjective, and even another adverb.

The following sections demonstrate the two different kinds of adverbs. It also shows you how to create adverbs from adjectives by following a set pattern.

Focusing on the two categories of adverbs

In Italian, adverbs fall into two categories:

>> **Original:** These adverbs aren't derived from other words. For example: **bene** *(well)*.

>> **Derived:** These adverbs are derived from adjectives. For example: **fortunatamente** *(luckily, fortunately)*, from the adjective **fortunato** *(lucky, fortunate)*.

Original adverbs

Original adverbs don't have a fixed form, so you're forced to simply learn them while you go. Table 4-6 includes some important adverbs.

TABLE 4-6 **Frequently Used Adverbs**

Adverb	Meaning	Adverb	Meaning
abbastanza	enough/rather	no	no
adesso/ora	now	non	not
anche	also	oggi	today
ancora	still/yet	poco	too little
bene	well	presto	soon/early
davvero	really	purtroppo	unfortunately
domani	tomorrow	sempre	always
dopo	after	spesso	often
fa	ago	subito	at once/right away
già	already	tanto	so/so much
ieri	yesterday	tardi	late
lontano	far	troppo	too much
mai/non . . . mai	ever/never	vicino	near
male	badly		

I may be giving you an abundance of new vocabulary. Choose which words are most useful to you and commit them to memory with whatever method works best.

Molto is an adjective meaning *much/many/a lot of*; it's also an adverb (invariable) meaning *very.* So, it can be used as an adjective or adverb.

Here are examples of **molto** as an adjective:

>> **molta acqua** *(a lot of water)*
>> **molti ravioli** *(many ravioli)*
>> **molto pane** *(a lot of bread)*
>> **molte lasagne** *(a lot of lasagna)*

And here's **molto** playing the role of adverb:

>> **Gli gnocchi sono molto buoni.** *(The gnocchi are very good.)*
>> **Mangiamo molto.** *(We eat a lot.)*

TIP

Adverbs are invariable and never agree!

Other common Italian adjectives that are also adverbs include **tanto, troppo,** and **poco.**

Derived adverbs

You form most derived adverbs in Italian by taking the singular form of an adjective and adding **–mente** (the equivalent of *–ly* in English) to it. Here are the basic rules for forming these adverbs, followed by some examples:

>> Adjectives that end in **-o**:
  • First, turn the **-o** to an **-a** the (feminine singular form of the adjective)
  • Then, add **–mente.**

  For example, **curioso** *(curious)* becomes **curiosamente** *(curiously)* and **chiaro** *(clear)* becomes **chiaramente** *(clearly)*.

>> Adjectives that end in **-e**: Simply add **-mente** to that adjective.

  For example, **dolce** *(sweet)* becomes **dolcemente** *(sweetly)*.

>> Adjectives that end in **-le** or **-re**: Drop the **-e** before adding **-mente**.

  For example, **facile** *(easy)* becomes **facilmente** *(easily)*; **regolare** *(regular/usual)* becomes **regolarmente** *(usually)*.

Note the following examples, where I show you the three forms in action:

Adjective	Adverb
certo	**Vuoi un dolce? Certamente!** *(Would you like some dessert?/Certainly!)*
veloce	**Parlano troppo velocemente!** *(They speak too quickly!)*
gentile	**Ha risposto gentilmente.** *(He/She answered kindly.)*

Table 4-7 includes key adjectives that you can transform into as adverbs by adding **–mente** + the rules for the three types:

TABLE 4-7 Adjectives Transformed into Adverbs

Adjective	Meaning	Adverb	Meaning
chiaro	*clear*	chiaramente	*clearly*
comodo	*comfortable*	comodamente	*comfortably*
difficile	*difficult*	difficilmente	*difficulty*
facile	*easy*	facilmente	*easily*
forte	*strong*	fortemente	*strongly*
fortunato	*fortunate, lucky*	fortunatamente	*fortunately/luckily*
giusto	*just/correct*	giustamente	*justly/correctly*
intelligente	*intelligent*	intelligentemente	*intelligently*
leggero	*light*	leggermente	*lightly*
onesto	*honest*	onestamente	*honestly*
semplice	*simple*	semplicemente	*simply*
sicuro	*sure*	sicuramente	*surely*
veloce	*fast, quick*	velocemente	fast, quickly

Finding a place for adverbs in a sentence

In general, you place most adverbs close to the words that they modify — that is, before the adjective and the noun or after the verb. Here are a couple of examples (note that the adverbs are **spesso** and **molto**):

> **Roberto va spesso in bici.** *(Robert often rides his bike.)*
>
> **Il concerto è molto bello.** *(The concert is very nice.)*

With compound tenses, such as the **passato prossimo** (see Chapter 6), you need to position adverbs differently, between the helping verb and the past participle.

TIP

When negating with adverbs, **non** *(not)* precedes the verb, and **mai** *(never)*, **ancora** *(still, yet)*, or **più** *(more)* follows it:

> **»** **Non mangio più il carpaccio.** *(I don't eat carpaccio anymore.)*

REMEMBER

Ancora also means *some more* or *again*. Regardless of meaning, its placement after a verb remains the same:

> **È ancora presto per telefonargli.** *(It's still too early to call him/them.)*
>
> **Vuoi ancora del gelato?** *(Do you want some more ice cream?)*

Comparing with the Comparative and Superlative

People make comparisons all of the time, in both English and Italian. This section explores the different ways you can use adjectives and adverbs to make comparisons and express superlatives. I divide this section into three kinds of comparisons:

» **Comparative:** You can break this down into three more types:

- The comparative of equality (=)
- The comparative of greater than (+)
- The comparative of less than (–)

>> **Superlative:** There are two different kinds of superlative:

- The **superlativo relativo** *(relative superlative)* that means *the most, and the least,* relative to a whole or to a group

- The **superlativo assoluto** *(absolute superlative)* that means *very, super,* or *very very*

>> **Irregular comparatives and superlatives:** These break down to irregular comparatives and irregular superlatives of specific adjectives and adverbs.

Comparing

The following sections discuss the rules for establishing comparisons in Italian. In both English and Italian, you use a comparative to compare and contrast in one of three ways:

>> **The comparative of equality:** Describing two similar items *(as much as)*; I indicate a comparative of equality with an equal sign (=) in this chapter.

>> **The comparative of greater than:** Say something is more than *(bigger, better, faster, prettier than)*, using the word **più** *(more)*; indicated with a plus sign (+) in this chapter.

>> **The comparative of less than:** Say something is less than *(smaller, worse, slower, uglier than)*, using the word **meno** *(less)*; denoted throughout this chapter with a negative sign (–).

You can convey the comparative in relation to names, nouns, pronouns, adjectives, infinitives, prepositional phrases, adverbs, and verbs.

Comparison of equality

To say that one object possesses a quality equal to another object, you use these expressions:

>> **(così) . . . come** *(as . . . as)*

>> **(tanto) . . . quanto** *(as much . . . as/as many . . . as)*

You must use **tanto . . . quanto** when comparing a quantity, and it agrees with the noun it precedes (if there is a noun); you must also use it with a verb.

For example:

> **Gina è (così) studiosa come Lisa.** *(Gina is as studious as Lisa.)* (The **così** is considered redundant and can be omitted, as is the **tanto**, hence I indicate it in parentheses.)
>
> **Bianca è (tanto) intelligente quanto Silvia.** *(Bianca is as intelligent as Silvia.)*
>
> **Compriamo tante pere quante mele.** *(We'll buy as many pears as apples.)* Note that **tante** and **quante** agree in gender and number with the nouns they modify.

Comparisons of greater than or less than

Unlike English, which adds *-er* to an adjective, as in *happy > happier,* to make a comparison, Italian doesn't add endings to adjectives or adverbs to create comparisons. For example, **vecchio** (*old*) remains the same, and you add the words **più** (**più vecchio**, *older*) or **meno** (**meno vecchio**, *less old*) before it:

> **Io sono più vecchia della mia amica Laura.** *(I am older than my friend Laura.)*

But the story doesn't end there. There are furthermore two ways of saying that one object has a quality more than or less than another object:

>> **più** (+) or **meno** (–) + **di** (*than*): **Io sono più bassa di te.** (*I'm shorter than you.*)

>> **più** (+) or **meno** (–) + **che** (*than*): **Io sono più bassa che alta.** (*I'm shorter than I am tall.*)

Here are other ways to make comparisons you need to know.

USING DI AND CHE

Be careful! Both **di** and **che** translate as *than.* These tips in context help you identify which version to use:

>> **di:** When the second term in a comparison is a proper noun, a pronoun without a preposition, a noun, or an adverb (see the later section "Putting Things Together with Prepositions" for how to contract the preposition **di**)

>> **che:** When you're comparing two identical parts of speech (two adjectives, two adverbs, two prepositional phrases, or two verbs)

Here are some examples of sentences that use **di** and what term is being compared:

>> Proper noun (**Rosa**): **Diana è più intelligente di Rosa.** *(Diana is more intelligent/smarter than Rosa.)*

>> Preposition with stressed pronoun (**te**): **Mangio più di te.** *(I eat more than you.)*

>> Adverb (**ieri**): **Sembri meno nervoso di ieri.** *(You seem less nervous than yesterday.)*

>> Noun (**cappuccino**): **L'espresso costa meno del cappuccino.** *(Espresso costs less than the cappuccino.)*

You must use **che** if you're comparing two identical parts of speech (nouns, verbs, adjectives, prepositional phrases, and so on):

>> Adjectives (**studiosa; divertente**): **Annamaria è più studiosa che divertente.** *(Annamaria is more studious than fun.)*

>> Verbs (**sciare; nuotare**): **Gli piace più sciare che nuotare.** *(He likes skiing more than swimming.)*

>> Prepositional phrases: (**a casa, al ristorante**): **Preferiamo cenare più a casa che al ristorante.** *(We prefer to have supper more at home than at the restaurant.)*

>> Nouns (**carne; pesce**): **Mangi meno carne che pesce.** *(You eat less meat than fish.)*

USING SEMPRE PIÙ AND SEMPRE MENO

When you want to say that something keeps increasing or decreasing — as in *more and more tired, taller and taller* — in Italian, you use the always-invariable **sempre più** (literally, *always more*) and **sempre meno** (literally, *always less*) + an adjective, an adverb, or a noun:

Fa sempre più freddo. *(It's getting colder and colder.)*

Designating the best and the worst with the superlatives

Just like in English, in Italian, you can rank objects to establish which one is the highest or the lowest in a series or group. The relative superlative and the absolute superlative allow you to express comparisons between two or more things and to describe the level of intensity of some qualities.

It's all relative

The *relative superlative* is the first of the two kinds of superlatives. To construct a sentence with the relative superlative (relative to a whole), you use **il/la più/il/la meno . . . di/in** (*the most/the least . . . of/in*). The adjective should agree with the noun that it refers to, as in the two following examples:

> **Luciano è il più alto dei figli.** *(Luciano is the tallest of the children.)*

> **Marta è la meno brava della squadra.** *(Marta is the least capable on the team.)*

And, you can also add on. Here's a formula that usually works:

> Subject + Verb + Object + **più/meno** + Adjective + **di** (contracted, if necessary) + Whole

So here are two examples:

> **Pepe's ha la pizza più buona di New Haven.** *(Pepe's has the best pizza in New Haven.)*

> **Mocca è il cane più dolce della casa.** *(Mocca is the sweetest dog in the house.)*

The absolute superlative

The *absolute superlative* expresses a lot of something, often translated as *very*, or even as *very very*.

TIP

To express the absolute superlative in Italian, you can simply add the adverb **molto** to an adjective or adverb, such as **I ragazzi sono molto veloci!** *(The kids are really fast!).* Or, you can add more pizzazz by dropping the final vowel of an adjective and adding **-issimo, -issima, -issimi,** or **-issime,** which agrees in gender and number with the noun. Table 4-8 shows some examples.

TABLE 4-8 **Forming the Absolute Superlative**

Adjective/Adverb	Absolute Superlative
ragazzo gentile *(kind boy)*	**ragazzo gentilissimo** *(very kind boy)*
ricette facili *(easy recipes)*	**ricette facilissime** *(very easy recipes)*
Nina parla bene l'italiano! *(Nina speaks Italian well!)*	**Nina parla benissimo l'italiano!** *(Nina speaks Italian very well!)*
	Note that **molto** in this sentence is an adverb and therefore doesn't agree.

REMEMBER

When an adjective or adverb ends in **-i,** it only adds **-ssimo.** For example, **È tardi!** *(It's late!)* becomes **È tardissimo!** *(It's very late!).*

Making irregular comparisons

In Italian, you have two ways of saying that someone or something is better or worse by using the adjectives **buono/migliore** *(good)* or **cattivo/peggiore** *(bad).* Similarly, you have two ways of saying if someone is **grande/maggiore** *(old/big)* or **piccolo/minore** *(young/little).* You can add **più** *(more)* or **meno** *(less)* to the adjective or use special words as listed in Table 4-9.

TABLE 4-9 **Comparatives and Superlatives of Adjectives with Special Forms**

Adjective	Comparative	Relative Superlative	Absolute Superlative
buono *(good)*	**più buono/ migliore** *(better)*	**il più buono** *(the best),* **il migliore** *(the best)*	**buonissimo/ottimo** *(very good)*
cattivo *(bad)*	**più cattivo/ peggiore** *(worse)*	**il più cattivo** *(the worst)* **il peggiore** *(the worst)*	**cattivissimo/pessimo** *(very bad)*

Focus on recognizing the differences between using an adjective or an adverb to say *better* (**migliore/meglio**) and *worse* (**peggiore/peggio**).

In all other respects, you use these special forms in the same way that you use the other comparatives:

> **Penso che il parmigiano sia migliore della fontina./Penso che il parmigiano sia più buono della fontina.** *(I think that parmesan is better than fontina.)*

Note: **Migliore** (+) and **peggiore** (−) are **-e** adjectives, and thus only have two forms as shown here (check out Chapter 7 for a discussion of the types of adjectives):

Gender and Number	Forms of migliore	Forms of peggiore
m/f, sing.	migliore	peggiore
m/f, pl.	migliori	peggiori

Here's an example using the appropriate form of **migliore**:

> **Chi sono le tue migliori amiche?** *(Who are your best [girl]friends?)*

With the adverbs **bene** (*well*) and **male** (*badly*), you have special forms only to express the comparatives and absolute superlatives of these qualities. I list them in Table 4-10.

TABLE 4-10 Comparatives and Superlatives of Adverbs with Special Forms

Adverb	Comparative	Absolute Superlative
bene *(well)*	**meglio** *(better)*	**benissimo** *(very well)*
male *(badly)*	**peggio** *(worse)*	**malissimo** *(very badly)*

The following examples puts these forms into practice:

> **Mio marito dice che gli italiani guidano meglio degli americani, ma non sono d'accordo. Guidano malissimo!**

(My husband says that Italians drive better than Americans, but I don't agree. They drive terribly!)

Chi canta peggio, tu o tua sorella? *(Who sings worse, you or your sister?)*

Putting Things Together with Prepositions

Prepositions are words that you need to link other words in a sentence in order to create fuller sentences. Prepositions are difficult to learn in any language because their use is often *idiomatic,* meaning native to the language but not obvious in translation. The basic rule, therefore, is practice, practice, and more practice.

In this section, I give you some preposition guidelines. I show you the main Italian prepositions (called **preposizioni semplici** or *simple prepositions*). I also show you how to combine (or contract) five simple prepositions with the definite articles in what's called **la preposizione articolata** *(the articulated preposition),* what I call the contracted preposition in this chapter.

Exploring the simple guys

Italian has some very common prepositions whose meanings often correspond to English. I list them here, starting with the most-frequently used. I give you the English translations that reflect the Italian prepositions' meanings, but remember that you can't assume that you'll use the same preposition in Italian and English every time.

REMEMBER

Italian has many more prepositions than I cover in this book. Consider this list a greatest hits of prepositions:

>> **di** *(of/about/some)*

>> **a** *(at/to)*

>> **da** *(from/by)*

>> **in** *(in/into/to/by)*

>> **su** *(on/onto)*

>> **con** *(with)*

>> **per** *(for/through/in order to)*

>> **fra/tra** *(between/among)*

Sometimes, the prepositions do translate neatly into English and aren't contracted! Note the following simple examples:

Flavia abita in Italia. *(Flavia lives in Italy.)*

Ricevo una mail da mia madre ogni giorno. *(I receive an email from my mother every day.)*

Vado a scuola con Rachele di solito. *(I usually go to school with Rachele.)*

Hai qualcosa per me? *(Do you have something for me?)*

Stressed pronouns generally follow prepositions. These are **me** (me), **te** (you), **sè** *(him/her/itself)*, **lui** (him), **lei** (her), **noi** (us), **voi** (you), **sè** *(themselves)*, **loro** *(them)*.

By the way, a great song by Lucio Battisti (**"Penso a te"**) can help you embed this structure in your mind, and you can practice your listening and speaking at the same time.

Contracting prepositions with articles and nouns

In this section, I show you how to contract the five most common prepositions with the seven definite articles, which agree in gender and number with nouns. (Check out Chapter 2 for more on definite articles). So, for example, you need to remember whether a noun is masculine, feminine, singular, or plural, and what article it takes. These contracted prepositions all follow a pattern, which you can see in Table 4-11.

TABLE 4-11 Prepositions Combined with Articles

Definite Article	di	a	da	in	su
il	del	al	dal	nel	sul
lo	dello	allo	dallo	nello	sullo
la	della	alla	dalla	nella	sulla
l'	dell'	all'	dall'	nell'	sull'
i	dei	ai	dai	nei	sui
gli	degli	agli	dagli	negli	sugli
le	delle	alle	dalle	nelle	sulle

For example, contract **di** + a definite article:

>> **di + il = del**

   Del becomes the stem for you to carry through for the other six articles, as in the first column in Table 4-11. Read these aloud to yourself to help yourself remember them and to connect them to the other prepositions.

>> **in + il = nel**

   Nel then becomes the stem that you can combine with the other six articles, as in the fourth column in Table 4-11.

General rules can help you familiarize yourself with prepositions regarding usage, and some verbs are typically followed by specific prepositions.

Going places: a or in

These guidelines show you when to use the preposition **a** or the preposition **in** when talking about going somewhere:

>> **a:** In front of **isole piccole** *(small islands)*, **città** *(cities)*

   ● Small island: **Andiamo a Capri.** *(Let's go to Capri.)*

   ● City: **Vado a New Orleans.** *(I'm going to New Orleans.)*

>> **in:** In front of **paesi** *(countries)*, **regioni** *(regions)*, **stati** *(states)*, **isole grandi** *(large islands)*

   ● Country: **Andiamo prima in Italia e poi in Grecia a marzo.** *(We're going first to Italy and then to Greece in March.)*

   ● Large island and region: **Quando andate in Sardegna?** *(When are you going to Sardegna?)*

In is almost never contracted with the article in front of a country:

Abito in Danimarca. *(I live in Denmark.)*

But if the country name is plural, you use an article:

Abitiamo negli Stati Uniti. *(We live in the United States.)*

The preposition **a** (*to/at*) is also frequently used with certain verbs, even though it might not translate as *at* or *to* in English. Note this sample sentence:

> **rispondere** *(to answer/respond)*: **Rispondo subito al telefono.** *(I'm going to answer the phone right away.)*

For holidays or named days and months, use **a** (*at/in*):

» **a Pasqua** *(at Easter)*

» **a febbraio** *(in February)*

Working with andare

The verb **andare** *(to go)* can be followed by several prepositions, depending on what you're trying to say (these prepositions aren't contracted):

> **Vado a casa.** *(I'm going home.)*
>
> **Vado in Argentina.** *(I'm going to Argentina.)*
>
> **Vado da Stefania.** *(I'm going to Stefania's place.)*
>
> **Vado con Stefania.** *(I'm going with Stefania.)*

Noting the many uses of da

You frequently use **da** with the verb **ricevere** *(to receive)*, although you can use it with other verbs and nous. Here's the formula for using **da** with **ricevere**:

> **ricevere una mail/una telefonata/un bacio/un regalo . . . da** = *to receive an email, a phone call, a kiss, a present . . . from.*

Note the following examples and how the preposition agrees with the noun:

> **Ho ricevuto un regalo dagli studenti italiani.** *(I received a present from the Italian students.)*
>
> **Riceviamo una telefonata da mio fratello.** *(We receive an email from my brother.)*

Da isn't contracted in this last sentence because a singular family relative doesn't take an article.

Chapter 2 shows you how to contract the preposition **a** in the context of saying **a che ora** (*at what time* something happens). Here are some examples that demonstrate more on how to say what time you do things. When you use the preposition **da** in the context of time (and place), it means *from*, just as it does in English:

> **Ceniamo dalle 20:00 alle 21:00.** *(Let's have/We're having supper from 8:00 to 9:00 p.m.)*

Figuring out the Italian ins

The preposition **in** (*in*) contracts with the Italian definite article to translate as *in/in the*. English has one way of saying that, but Italian has seven! The verb **mettere** *(to put/to place)* is frequently used with the preposition **in.**

Note the following examples, which illustrate all seven forms. Each of the sentences begins as follows: **Metto lo zucchero** (*I'm putting the sugar in . . .*).

> **Metto lo zucchero nel tè.** *(I'm putting/I put sugar in [the] tea.)*
>
> . . . **nella limonata.** *(in the lemonade.)*
>
> . . . **nei biscotti.** *(in the cookies.)*
>
> . . . **nelle paste.** *(in the pastries.)*
>
> . . . **nel pane.** *(in the bread.)*

Using di for possession and the partitive

The preposition **di** has two prominent uses:

>> To show possession of something

>> To show an indefinite quantity (known as a *partitive* construction), translated as *some*

REMEMBER

In English, for possession, you add an apostrophe and *s* to a noun or a name. In Italian, you use **di**: **Il libro di Teresa** literally translates as *the book of Teresa*, but common English usage translates as *Teresa's book*. You also use a possessive adjective, such as *his* or *her*: **il suo gatto** translates as *his/her cat*. (See Chapter 2 for more on possessive adjectives.) Get a handle on the possessive **di** in the following set (the possibilities are endless):

> **Questo è il libro del ragazzo.** *(This is the boy's book.)*
>
> **... di Luigi.** (*Luigi's:* No article necessary with a proper noun.)
>
> **... degli studenti.** *(the students'.)*
>
> **... dei miei studenti.** *(my students'.)*

Using the partitive

Italian commonly uses the preposition **di** + definite article + noun as the partitive, which simply means *some*. You need to know noun number and gender to effectively use this structure. Use the singular partitive for uncountable things (**del, dell', della, dello**) and the plural partitive for countable things (**dei, degli, delle**). The singular partitive identifies an indeterminate amount of something, such as water, bread, and patience. For example:

> **Prendo del burro e degli spaghetti.** *(I'm getting some butter and some spaghetti.)*

Putting su on the spot

The preposition **su** usually means *on*. It generally translates literally into English. So, if you want to say *The cat is on the car* in Italian, you'd say **Il gatto è sulla macchina.**

REMEMBER

If you're talking about doing something on a certain day, you don't use **su**, just use the name of the day. For example, **Giochi a tennis sabato?** (*Are you going to play tennis <u>on</u> Saturday?*)

Noting the exceptions

Italian has so many idiomatic uses of prepositions that I can't list them all. These oddball forms don't follow the same contracted preposition guidelines that I discuss throughout the section

"Putting Things Together with Prepositions." Therefore, you must memorize them. Nonetheless, you can look for patterns. For example, most means of transportation take the preposition **in** and no definite article, when conveying the notion *by*

> **Vado in traghetto (in macchina, in aereo).** *(I'm going by ferry [car, plane].)*

Some specific places also take **in** and no definite article:

> **Vado in biblioteca.** *(I'm going to the library.)*
>
> **Sono in biblioteca.** *(I'm in the library.)*

Here are additional terms that don't require definite articles. Many of them, but not all, are places and means of transportation:

>> **in macchina** *(by car)*, **in treno** *(by train)*, **in bici/in bicicletta** *(by bike)*, **in autobus** *(by bus)*, **in aereo** *(by plane)*, **in barca** *(by boat)*

>> **a cavallo** *(by horse)*, **a piedi** *(on foot)*

>> **a casa** *(to/at home)*

>> **in cucina** *(in/to the kitchen)*

>> **in centro** *(to/in the center of town)*

>> **in banca** *(to/in the bank)*

>> **a letto** *(to bed)*

>> **a teatro** *(to the theater)*

>> **a scuola** *(to school)*

>> **in montagna** *(to/in the mountains)*

>> **a tavola** *(to/at the table)*

>> **al cinema** *(to the movies)*

>> **a mezzanotte** *(at midnight)*

>> **sul giornale** *(in the newspaper)*

>> **su Internet** *(on the internet)*

>> **alla radio** *(on the radio)*

>> **alla televisione** *(on television)*

>> **in vacanza** *(on vacation)*

Chapter **5**

Asking and Answering Questions

You never know when you're going to strike up a conversation with your recently acquired Italian pen pal, look for a partner on a dating app, or meet your new neighbors. Asking and answering questions are key to communication in any language. Sometimes when you ask a question, all you need is a "yes" or "no" response. Other times, you might need to ask for, and provide, more information.

For this reason, this chapter shows you how to ask simple questions and how to answer questions affirmatively or negatively. It also breaks down the *interrogative adjectives and pronouns* (or question words), such as **chi?** *(who?)*, such as **dove?** *(where?)*, **come** *(how?)*, **perché** *(why)*, **quando** *(when)*, **quanto** *(how much)*, and **quale?** *(which/what?)*. And, we also show you how to point things out with the demonstrative adjectives **questo** *(this/these)* and **quello** *(that/those)*.

Questioning Basics: What You Need to Know

Asking a question is pretty straightforward in Italian. You can alter the intonation or inflection of your voice: the declarative sentence **Mangi** (*You're eating*) becomes **Mangi?** (*Are you eating?*), simply by adding a questioning tone to your voice. Here I answer that question.

When answering a question in the affirmative, you can add **sì** (*yes*), or you can simply use the verb:

> **Sì, mangio.** (*Yes, I'm eating.*)
>
> **Mangio.** (*I'm eating.*)

When answering in the negative, you may simply say:

> **No.** (*No.*)
>
> **Non mangio.** (*I'm not eating.*)
>
> **No, non mangio.** (*No, I am not eating.*)

REMEMBER

The **non** is necessary, but the **no** in the third answer is optional because all you need to make the sentence negative is the **non**.

Another tactic for posing a question is by reversing the word order, placing the subject at the end of the sentence (although this order isn't always necessary):

> **Chiara è italiana** (*Chiara is Italian*) becomes a question with **È italiana Chiara?** (*Is Chiara Italian?*)

To answer in the affirmative, you say:

> **Chiara è italiana.** (*Chiara is Italian.*)

To answer in the negative, you say:

> **Chiara non è italiana.** (*Chiara isn't Italian.*)

If you want to ask *why don't you (we, you all . . .)/don't you* begin the sentence with **non** (well, sort of):

> **Perchè non andiamo al cinema stasera?** (Why don't we go to the movies tonight?)

> **Non vuoi una bella fetta di cocomero?** *(Don't you want a nice piece of watermelon?)*

The **non** can also mean *aren't you?* For example, **Non mangi?** translates to *Aren't you eating?*

REMEMBER

In Italian, when posing a question, there's no word for *is, are, do,* or *does,* under certain circumstances, as the following samples show:

REMEMBER

>> **Lui va al cinema?** *(Is he going to the movies?)*

>> **Vai al concerto?** *(Are you going to the concert?)*

>> **Hanno posto per me nella macchina?** *(Do they have room for me in the car?)*

Tackling Those Interrogatives

This section walks you through the interrogative adjectives and pronouns and provides you with sample sentences for many of the most commonly used ones. Table 5-1 lists the interrogative adjectives and pronouns, as well as their meanings.

TABLE 5-1 Interrogative Adjectives and Pronouns

Interrogative	English	Example
chi	*who*	**Chi è quello?** *(Who's that (man)?)*
quando	*when*	**Quando torni?** *(When are you coming back?)*
perché	*why*	**Perché studi l'italiano?** *(Why are you studying Italian?)*
quanto/a	*how much*	**Quanta acqua bevi**? *(How much water do you drink?)*

(continued)

TABLE 5-1 *(continued)*

Interrogative	English	Example
quanti/ quante	*how many*	**Quante persone vengono?** *(How many people are coming?)*
cosa	*what*	**Cosa dici?** *(What are you saying? / What do you say?)*
che cosa	*what*	**Che cosa è questo?** *(What is this?)*
che + noun	*what*	**Che giorno è oggi?** *(What day is today?)*
dove	*where*	**Dove vivi?** *(Where do you live?)*
dov'è	*where is*	**Dov'è Piazza Garibaldi?** *(Where is Piazza Garibaldi?)* **Dove sei?** *(Where are you?)*
dove sono	*where are*	**Dove sono le Tremiti?** *(Where are the Tremiti Islands?)*
come	*how*	**Come stai?** *(How are you?)* **Come si dice *peach* in italiano?** *(How do you say peach in Italian?)* **Come ti chiami?** *(What's your name?)*
com'è	*How is/What is something like*	**Com'è il tuo uomo ideale?** *(What's your ideal man like?)* **Come sono gli spaghetti?** *(How's the spaghetti?)*
quale	*what/which*	**Quale dei due preferisci?** *(Which of the two do you prefer?)*
qual è	*what is*	**Qual è il tuo ristorante preferito?** *(What's your favorite restaurant?)*
quali sono	*what are*	**Quali sono i giorni della settimana?** *(What are the days of the week?)*

REMEMBER

Che, che cosa, and **cosa** are interchangeable when they mean *what* and are followed by a verb. For example:

Che cosa?/Che?/Cosa fai nel tempo libero? *(What do you do in your free time?)*

You never include the interrogative adjective or pronoun in your answer (just like you don't in English):

Dove vai dopo la lezione? *(Where are you going after class?)*

Vado a casa. *(I'm going home.)*

You don't need **dove** in the preceding response.

The one exception, although it's not really an exception, is when you use **perché,** which means both *why* and *because:*

Perché non vai al mare? *(Why don't you go to the beach?)*

Perché non mi va. *(Because I don't feel like it.)*

When you say **perché non . . .?**, it means you're also making a suggestion. Think of how, in English, you'd use the words, *Why don't . . .?*

Cosa facciamo? *(What should we do?)*

Perché non andiamo a prendere un gelato? *(Why don't we go get an ice cream?)*

Table 5-2 shows some sample answers to questions. I put some optional words in parentheses — the sentence makes sense without them, but you could add them for clarification.

TABLE 5-2 Answering Questions

Question	Translation	Answer	Translation
Chi è quello?	Who is that?	(Lui) È mio cugino.	He's my cousin.
Quando torni?	When are you coming back?	(Torno) A settembre.	(I'm coming back) in September.
Perché studi l'italiano?	Why do you study Italian?	(Studio l'italiano) Perché mi piace.	(I study Italian) because I like it.
Quanto costa l'albergo?	How much does the hotel cost?	Costa 600 euro.	It costs 600 euros.
Quanti anni hai?	How old are you?	Ho venticinque anni.	I'm 25.

(continued)

TABLE 5-2 *(continued)*

Question	Translation	Answer	Translation
Quante persone vengono?	*How many people are coming?*	**Vengono diciassette persone.**	*Seventeen people are coming.*
Che cosa/Che/ Cosa è questo?	*What is this?*	**È un pesce.**	*It's a fish.*
Che giorno è oggi?	*What day is today?*	**(Oggi) È sabato.**	*(Today) is Saturday.*
Dove vivi?	*Where do you live?*	**(Vivo) A Fairfield.**	*(I live) in Fairfield.*
Dov'è Piazza Garibaldi?	*Where is Piazza Garibaldi?*	**È in centro.**	*It's downtown.*
Dove sei?	*Where are you?*	**(Sono) In macchina.**	*(I'm) in the car.*
Di dove sei?	*Where are you from?*	**(Sono di) Frosinone.**	*(I'm from) Frosinone.*
Dove sono le chiavi?	*Where are the keys?*	**(Le chiavi sono) Sul tavolo.**	*(The keys are) on the table.*
Come stai?	*How are you?*	**Sto benissimo, grazie! E tu?**	*I'm super, thanks! And you?*
Come si dice *peach* in italiano?	*How do you say peach in Italian?*	**Si dice pesca.**	*You say pesca.*
Com'è il tuo uomo ideale?	*What is your ideal man like?*	**(Il mio uomo ideale) È onesto, moro, gentile, sportivo e intelligente.**	*(My ideal man) is honest, dark-haired, kind, athletic, and smart.*
Come sei?	*What are you like?*	**Sono bassa e pigra.**	*I'm short and lazy.*
Come sono gli spaghetti?	*How's the spaghetti?*	**(Gli spaghetti sono) Ottimi!**	*(The spaghetti is/are) great!*
Quale dei due preferisci?	*Which of the two do you prefer?*	**(Preferisco) Quello.**	*(I prefer) that one.*
Qual è il tuo ristorante preferito?	*What's your favorite restaurant?*	**(Il mio ristorante preferito è) La Ca' de Vèn.**	*(My favorite restaurant is) La Ca' de Vèn.*
Quali sono i giorni della settimana?	*What are the days of the week?*	**(I giorni della settimana sono) lunedì, martedì . . .**	*(The days of the week are) Monday, Tuesday . . .*

TIP

You might need some possessive adjectives — **il mio** *(my)* or **il tuo** *(your)* — to formulate a complete response when answering certain questions, such as **Chi sono i tuoi attori preferiti?** *(Who are your favorite actors?).* Check out Chapter 2 for all your possessive adjective needs.

The following sections show you how some of the Interrogatives can be combined with the verb **essere** *(to be).* These combined forms are frequently used, so it is useful to chunk them here.

Making more out of some interrogatives

In Italian, you can truncate some of the interrogatives and combine them with the verb **essere** *(to be).* These sections walk you through how to use the interrogatives **dove** *(where),* **come** *(how),* and **quale** *(which),* and also how to make the expressions **c'è** *(there is)* and **ci sono** *(there are)* work for you as both questions and answers.

Dove e come

The interrogatives **dove** and **come** can be contracted with the verb **essere** *(to be)* in whatever person you're referring to. For example, here are these interrogatives with third person singular and third person plural verbs. When adopting the third person singular, contract the **dove** to **dov-**, and the **come** to **com-**. Then, add an apostrophe plus the verb **essere** in the third person singular **è**, as follows:

> **Dov'è Mario.** *(Where's Mario?)*
>
> **Dove sono i ragazzi?** *(Where are the boys/kids?)*
>
> **Com'è quel ristorante?** *(How is that restaurant?* or *What's that restaurant like?)*
>
> **Come sono gli gnocchi?** *(How are the gnocchi?)*

Of course, you may also combine **dove** and **come** with the other persons of essere:

> **Ragazzi, dove siete?** *(Hey guys,where are you?)*

Com'è, **Come sei,** and **come sono** ask what something/someone is like, <u>not</u> how they're doing.

Quale

Use **quale** in the singular, **quali** in the plural, but **qual è** when combined with the third person singular of **essere:**

> **Quale film vuoi vedere?** *(What/which film do you want to see?)*

> **Qual è il mare più profondo in Italia?** *(What is the deepest sea in Italy?)*

> **Quali amici hai invitato?** *(Which friends did you invite?)*

C'è and ci sono

Although seemingly insignificant, you just can't get around in Italian without the essential terms **c'è** *(there is/is there?)* and **ci sono** *(there are/are there?)* that are useful both for asking and answering questions. Just remember that both have a *ch* (as in *child*) sound:

> **Cosa c'è nel frigo?** *(What's in the fridge?)*

> **Chi non c'è a lezione oggi?** *(Who's not in class today?)*

> **C'è una mosca nella mia minestra!** *(There's a fly in my soup!)*

> **Ci sono ancora dei ravioli?** *(Are there any ravioli left?)*

> **Ci sono undici studenti nella classe.** *(There are 11 students in the class.)*

By itself, the question **Cosa c'è?** means *What's up?/What's wrong?* **C'è qualcosa che che non va?** is another way of asking what's wrong.

Taking care of basic needs

Sometimes you just need to ask for something very basic but necessary. Here are some phrases that will take you far:

> **Scusi, dov'è il bagno per favore?** *(Excuse me, where is the bathroom please?)*

> **Scusi, dov'è la farmacia più vicina?** *(Excuse me, where's the nearest pharmacy?)*

Non capisco. *(I don't understand.)*

Non lo so. *(I don't know.)*

Negating — Answering in the Negative

Many questions in Italian require you to say more than **no**, so this section shows you how to negate more complicated questions. Table 5-3 goes from a question to a negative answer and underlines the specific indefinite adjective–pronoun (in the affirmative) and also the negation.

TABLE 5-3 Answering in the Negative

Italian Question	English	Italian Response	English
Visiti la Sardegna?	*Are you visiting Sardegna?*	**No, <u>non</u> visito la Sardegna.**	*No, I'm not visiting Sardegna.*
Vai <u>sempre</u> a Matera?	*Do you always go to Matera?*	**<u>Non</u> vado <u>mai</u> a Matera.**	*I never go to Matera.*
Hai <u>ancora</u> parenti in Italia?	*Do you still have relatives in Italy?*	**No, <u>non</u> ho <u>più</u> parenti in Italia.**	*No, I no longer have relatives in Italy.*
Hai <u>già</u> visto Capri?	*Have you already seen Capri?*	**<u>Non</u> ho <u>ancora</u> visto Capri.**	*I haven't yet seen Capri.*
Conosci <u>qualcuno</u> a Bari?	*Do you know someone in Bari?*	**No, <u>non</u> conosco <u>nessuno</u> a Bari.**	*No, I don't know anyone in Bari.*
C'è <u>qualcosa</u> da fare qui?	*Is there anything to do here?*	**<u>Non</u> c'è <u>niente</u> da fare qui.**	*No, there's nothing to do here.*
Vedrai <u>tutti</u>?	*Will you see everyone?*	**No, <u>non</u> vedrò <u>nessuno</u>.**	*No, I won't see anyone.*

TIP

In Italian, unlike English, you may, and should, when appropriate, have several negation words in the same sentence. Also, the **non** is always necessary when negating (unless you begin the sentence with the negation, as in **Nessuno mi ama**! [*No one loves me!*]).

Pointing to Something with Questo and Quello

The demonstrative adjectives and pronouns **questo** *(this/these)* or **quello** *(that/those)* are versatile words that you use to point to people, things, and situations. You can use them to ask questions and to point things out.

You can use them as adjectives or pronouns.

>> **Adjectives:** When you add a noun after **questo** or **quello.**

>> **Pronouns:** When they refer to a noun, name, or pronoun that you've already mentioned.

When you use either **questo** or **quello,** make it agree in gender and number with the person or thing to which it refers.

REMEMBER   The following sections look closely at these two.

Questo (this/these)

Questo *(this/these)* acts like an adjective that has four possible endings, but it actually has five forms. Use **quest'** in front of a singular noun beginning with a vowel (refer to the following to explain when to use which form):

Gender	Adjective
Masc. sing.	**questo ristorante** *(this restaurant)*
Fem. sing.	**questa persona** *(this person)*
Masc. pl.	**questi uomini** *(these men)*
Fem. pl.	**queste poesie** *(these poems)*

Masc./Fem. with a singular noun beginning with vowel **quest'altro, quest'altra** *(this other thing/this other [male]/this other [female])*

As a pronoun, **questo** replaces the noun, while agreeing with it. It has four forms: **questo, questa, questi,** and **queste.**

For example:

> **Quali stivali prendi?** *(What boots are you getting?)*
>
> **Prendo questi.** *(I'm getting these.)*

Here are a few model sentences of **questo** as a demonstrative adjective and as a pronoun:

> Adjective: **Questo cantante è fantastico!** *(This singer is fantastic!)*
>
> Adjective: **Queste lasagne sono deliziose!** *(This lasagna is delicious!)* (**Lasagne** is almost always plural in Italian.)
>
> Pronoun: **Questa è mia madre.** *(This is my mother.)*
>
> Pronoun: **Che cos'è questo?** *(What's this?)*

Quello (that/those)

Quello *(that/those)* has seven forms when preceding a noun, which correspond to the seven definite articles when combined with a preposition (which you can read about in Chapters 2 and 4). The **quello** you use should agree in number and gender with the noun.

The following gives the forms for **quello** when used as a demonstrative adjective:

Italian	English
quel attore	*(that actor)*
quello studio	*(that office)*
quell'amico	*(that friend)*
quella storia	*(that story)*
quei pomodori	*(those tomatoes)*
quegli stivali	*(those boots)*
quelle sorelle	*(those sisters)*

Note the following questions with the demonstrative **quello,** which also works just like the adjective **bello.** The form that you use depends on the first letter of the noun that it precedes:

Chi è quell'uomo? *(Who is that man?)*

Chi è quel bell'uomo? *(Who is that beautiful man?)*

È tuo quello zaino? *(Is that backpack yours?)*

Di chi sono quei libri? *(Whose books are those?)*

When acting as a pronoun, **quello** behaves like the adjectives that have four endings: It agrees in number and gender with whatever it's substituting:

Gender	Adjective
Masc. sing.	**quello** *(that)*
Fem sing.	**quella** *(that)*
Masc. pl.	**quelli** *(those)*
Fem. pl.	**quelli** *(those)*

Here I take a look at a question using **quello** with one of the preceding seven adjective forms and answer it with a demonstrative pronoun:

Adjective: **Chi è quell'uomo?** *(Who is that man?)*

Pronoun: **Quello è mio padre.** *(That's my father.)*

You use the form **quelli/quelle** *(those ones/those who)* only as a pronoun:

Quelli non vogliono pagare il conto. *(Those* [people] *don't want to pay the bill.)*

Similar to **questo,** you can add an adjective instead of repeating a noun and an adjective:

Vuoi la giacca blu o quella verde? *(Do you want the blue or the green jacket?)*

Quella verde. *(The green one.)*

IN THIS CHAPTER

» **Unveiling the past with the** passato prossimo

» **Forming past participles**

» **Using the** passato prossimo

» **Getting familiar with the** imperfetto

» **Choosing between the** passato prossimo **and the** imperfetto

Chapter **6**

Talking about the Past

I n Italian, when you talk or write about the past, there are a couple of very common tenses, each with specific conjugations and uses.

The first past tense I look at in this chapter is the *present perfect tense*, or **passato prossimo**, which is the term I use in this book. Generally, you use the **passato prossimo** to talk about an action that has been completed in the past. For example, the phrase **Sono andata a casa** means *I went home*, no matter whether you went home two minutes ago or two months ago.

The second past tense, the *imperfect*, or **imperfetto,** generally indicates a past action or a state as uncompleted, continuous, or ongoing. The **imperfetto** is very common and indispensable for everyday speech, narrating, and reading. Frequently called the *past descriptive tense,* the **imperfetto** is often found in fairy tales and literature. For example, **C'era una volta una principessa** means *Once upon a time there was a princess.* The **imperfetto** tense has its own specific uses that set it apart from the **passato prossimo.**

In this chapter, you discover how to conjugate verbs in these two tenses and when to use them, with plenty of model sentences that show how to use them and how to decide if you need one or the other. I don't include the **passato remoto,** which is used primarily in historical narratives, because it lies outside the scope of this book.

Talking about the Past with the Passato Prossimo

The **passato prossimo** is the tense you use most frequently in everyday speech (and in emails and letters) to talk about what's happened in recent times. The following sections help you keep an eye on recent events by forming, conjugating, and using the **passato prossimo.** Along the way, you find out how to form regular and irregular past participles and how to determine which auxiliary verb you need. Soon, you'll be using the **passato prossimo** with ease.

REMEMBER

The **passato prossimo** is the tense that you use to refer to events that happened anywhere from 5 minutes ago to 50 years ago (even more). It specifically references an action begun and completed in the past:

Ho parlato con Carlo ieri. *(I spoke with Carlo yesterday.)*

The most important thing you need to know about the **passato prossimo** is that it's a *compound tense,* which means that it *always* has two parts:

>> An auxiliary verb

>> A past participle

To form the **passato prossimo,** you need the following:

>> The present tense of the helping verbs **avere** *(to have)* or **essere** *(to be):* (Refer to the section "Figuring Out Which Auxiliary to Use" later in this chapter for more information.)

>> The past participle: (The next section explains which past participle to use.)

Dealing with Regular and Irregular Past Participles

Because the past participle is such an essential part of the **passato prossimo** (and all the other compound tenses in Italian), I dedicate the next two sections to making a past participle out of an infinitive. Then, I circle back and combine them with their auxiliary verbs.

Forming regular past participles

When it comes to the past participle, most verbs — even those that are irregular in other tenses — form the past participle according to these rules.

Forming the regular past participle of -**are**, -**ere**, and -**ire** verbs is quite simple. Follow these steps:

1. **Take the infinitive of the verb.**

   For example, **parlare** *(to speak)*, **vendere** *(to sell)*, **capire** *(to undertand)*

2. **Cut the infinitive at its stem.**

   For example, **parl-, vend-, cap-**

3. **Add the appropriate ending.**

   - -**are** verbs = -**ato**
   - -**ere** verbs = -**uto**
   - -**ire** verbs = -**ito**

Table 6-1 shows you the three types of regular past participles. (For irregular past participles, see Table 6-2 and Table 6-3.)

TABLE 6-1 Creating Regular Past Participles

Infinitive	Stem	Past Participle
-**are**, like **parlare** *(to speak)*	**parl-**	**parlato** *(spoke/spoken)*
-**ere**, like **vendere** *(to sell)*	**vend-**	**venduto** *(sold)*
-**ire**, like **capire** *(to understand)*	**cap-**	**capito** *(understood)*

But how does the **passato prossimo** translate into English? It could be any of these ways, depending on context! Consider this example:

Hai parlato con tuo padre. *(You spoke with your father./You have spoken with your father./You did speak with your father.)*

Forming the past participle of irregular verbs

Italian has a whole slew of irregular past participles. In most cases, the stem of the verb changes by losing some letters — really, it contracts. Many irregular past participles are in the conjugation of -ere verbs.

Table 6-2 illustrates many common verbs with irregular past participles that use **avere** as their auxiliary verbs. As you go through this table, look for patterns in these irregular past participles that you can easily remember. Challenge yourself to memorize them by drilling with them on a site such as Quizlet or by creating your own flashcards (and check a dictionary when in doubt).

TABLE 6-2 Making Irregular Past Participle with Avere

Infinitive	Past Participle	Infinitive	Past Participle and Translation
ammettere *(to admit)*	**ammesso** *(admitted)*	**piangere** *(to cry)*	**pianto** *(cried)*
aprire *(to open)*	**aperto** *(opened)*	**prendere** *(to have, to take)*	**preso** *(took, have/has taken, had)*
bere *(to drink)*	**bevuto** *(drank, have/has drunk)*	**produrre** *(to produce)*	**prodotto** *(produced)*
chiedere *(to ask)*	**chiesto** *(asked)*	**promettere** *(to promise)*	**promesso** *(promised)*
commettere *(to commit)*	**commesso** *(committed)*	**ridere** *(to laugh)*	**riso** *(laughed)*
comporre *(to compose)*	**composto** *(composed)*	**rispondere** *(to answer)*	**risposto** *(answered)*

Infinitive	Past Participle	Infinitive	Past Participle and Translation
correggere *(to correct)*	corretto *(corrected)*	rompere *(to break)*	rotto *(broke, have/has broken)*
corrompere *(to corrupt)*	corrotto *(corrupted)*	scegliere *(to choose)*	scelto *(chose, have/has chosen)*
decidere *(to decide)*	deciso *(decided)*	scrivere *(to write)*	scritto *(wrote, have/has written)*
detrarre *(to detract)*	detratto *(detracted)*	soffrire *(to suffer)*	sofferto *(suffered)*
dipingere *(to paint)*	dipinto *(painted)*	sorridere *(to smile)*	sorriso *(smiled)*
dire *(to say)*	detto *(said)*	sottrare *(to subtract)*	sottratto *(subtracted)*
disporre *(to arrange)*	disposto *(arranged)*	spendere *(to spend)*	speso *(spent)*
dividere *(to divide, to split)*	diviso *(divided)*	spingere *(to push)*	spinto *(pushed)*
fare *(to do, to make)*	fatto *(did, done, made)*	stringere *(to squeeze, to shake hands)*	stretto *(squeezed, shook)*
leggere *(to read)*	letto *(read)*	tradurre *(to translate)*	tradotto *(translated)*
mettere *(to put)*	messo *(put)*	vedere *(to see)*	veduto, visto *(saw, have/has seen)*
offrire *(to offer, to treat)*	offerto *(offered, treated)*	vivere *(to live)*	vissuto *(lived)*
perdere *(to lose)*	perso, perduto *(lost)*	uccidere *(to kill)*	ucciso *(killed)*
permettere *(to allow, to permit)*	permesso *(allowed, permitted)*		

Two verbs have two interchangeable past participles. You can use either one, although the second option is more appropriate, modern, and in keeping with standard written and spoken Italian:

>> **perdere: perduto** and **perso**

>> **vedere: veduto** and **visto**

The past participle of the verb **fare** *(to do/to make)* keeps only the **f-** of the infinitive and doubles the **tto** become **fatto**. In that case, it's a little bit irregular. Furthermore, when answering a question, such as in the following example, you don't need **fatto** in your response:

Cosa hai fatto ieri sera? *(What did you do last night?)*

Ieri sera sono andata al mare con gli amici. *(Last night, I went to the beach with my friends.)*

The past participle of the verb **dare** *(to give)* is quite regular. It keeps the **d-** and becomes **dato:**

Hai dato i soldi alla mamma? *(Did you give Mom the money?/ Did you give the money to Mom?)*

Most verbs ending in **-scere** add an **i** before the past participle ending in order to preserve the soft *shh* sound of the infinitive. I indicate the transitive verbs (which take **avere**) with an **a.**, and the intransitive ones (which take **essere**) with an **e.**

For example, **conoscere,** *a. (to know)* becomes **conosciuto** *(known),* and **crescere,** *e. (to grow/to raise)* becomes **cresciuto** *(grown/raised).* But *not* **nascere,** *e. (to be born)*, which is **nato** *(born).*

Verbs ending in **-cere**, like **piacere,** *e. (to like)*, also take an **i** before adding the past participle ending, in order to keep a *ch* sound, as in **piaciuto** *(liked).*

Figuring Out Which Auxiliary to Use

The past participle is the second part of the **passato prossimo** (see the previous section). The first part is the helping, or auxiliary, verb **essere** or **avere**. But how do you know whether to use **avere** or **essere**?

REMEMBER

In Italian compound tenses like the **passato prossimo**, *transitive verbs* take the auxiliary verb **avere**, and *intransitive verbs* take the auxiliary verb **essere**. I cover **avere** and **essere** in the present tense in Chapter 3.

Here is how to form the **passato prossimo**:

> Present tense of **avere** *(to have)* or **essere** *(to be)* + the past participle

In order to form the **passato prossimo** of a particular verb, follow these steps:

1. **Choose an auxiliary verb.**

You use either **avere** or **essere**, depending on whether the verb is transitive or intransitive.

2. **Choose the ending of the past participle.**

The following sections explore which helping verb (**avere** or **essere**) to use when forming the **passato prossimo**.

Using avere in the passato prossimo

To create the **passato prossimo** with **avere** *(to have)*, you use the present tense of **avere: ho, hai, ha, abbiamo, avete, hanno** + the past participle (which ends in **-o** and is invariable) of the transitive verb. Check out this example:

> **Abbiamo visto il nuovo film di Cortellesi ieri sera.** *(We saw Cortellesi's new film last night.)*

Transitive verbs may almost always be followed by direct objects. For example, the verb **mangiare** *(to eat)* is transitive. You can say *I eat/I ate* without following the verb with a direct object, but you know that you can also say, *I eat gnocchi/I ate gnocchi.* The gnocchi, in this case, is the direct object, answering the question "Who?" or "What?"

mangiare *(to eat)*

io ho mangiato	noi abbiamo mangiato
tu hai mangiato	voi avete mangiato
lui, lei, Lei ha mangiato	loro hanno mangiato

Loro hanno mangiato a casa. *(They ate at home.)*

REMEMBER

For the purposes of this book, the past participle of transitive verbs ends in **o**. In Italian, a direct object pronoun can change the ending of the past participle, but you don't need to worry about that now.

There are a few exceptions: A few intransitive verbs, such as **dormire** *(to sleep)*, **pranzare/cenare** *(to dine)*, **parlare** *(to speak)*, and **telefonare** *(to phone)*, always take **avere**.

Using essere in the passato prossimo

Intransitive verbs don't take a direct object and use the verb **essere** as their helping verb. Unlike the transitive verbs whose past participles end in **o**, the past participle of intransitive verbs must agree in gender and number with the subject of the sentence; therefore, the past participle has four endings: **o**, **a**, **i**, and **e** (just like the adjectives that have four endings, which I talk about in Chapter 2).

Figure 6-1 helps you to visualize many of the intransitive verbs in the house of **essere**. You can associate this initial list of intransitive verbs with many things you do in a house — such as **venire** *(to come)*, **andare** *(to go)*, **uscire** *(to go out)*, **salire** *(to go up)*, **scendere** *(to go down)*, and so on. The whole category of reflexive verbs is also included in this figure.

All the verbs in Figure 6-1 are intransitive, and you conjugate them with the auxiliary verb **essere**. For example:

Sono partita alle 8:00 di mattina. *(I left at 8:00 in the morning.)*

La casa del verbo *essere*

nascere

all reflexive verbs

essere
sembrare
piacere
diventare

crescere

stare   rimanere   restare   vivere

correre

cadere

salire

scendere

morire

RIP

uscire
partire
andare

entrare
venire
tornare
arrivare

© *John Wiley & Sons, Inc.*

FIGURE 6-1: The Casa di Essere.
Note: Correre can take both essere and avere.

You'll have much success with the **passato prossimo** if you can memorize that intransitive verbs take **essere.**

All reflexive verbs take **essere** in the **passato prossimo** as well.

The following shows an example of an intransitive verb conjugated in the **passato prossimo.** Unlike verbs that take **avere,** you can see that the past participles agree with the subjects.

uscire *(to go out)*

io **sono uscito/a**	noi **siamo usciti/e**
tu **sei uscito/a**	voi **siete usciti/e**
lui, lei, Lei **è uscito/a**	loro **sono usciti/e**

Io sono uscita con Giancarlo ieri sera.
(I went out with Giancarlo last night.)

Take note of these other examples that illustrate the structure of intransitive verbs in the **passato prossimo:**

>> **Isabel and Sofia sono andate a New York.** *(Isabel a Sofia went to New York.)*

This past participle takes the feminine singular **-e** ending, to agree with the girls.

>> **Peter e Cathi sono andati in Spagna.** *(Peter and Cathi went to Spain.)*

If the gender in a sentence is unspecified, or if there's a masculine and a feminine subject, then the masculine ending takes precedence.

TIP

Table 6-3 provides some of the more commonly used intransitive verbs with their past participles. Note the structure and commonalities of the verbs in the **casa di essere** in Figure 6-1. Some of the past participles are *irregular,* which means they don't follow the regular **-ato, -uto, -ito** endings. Using these verbs is the best way to learn them.

TABLE 6-3 The House of Essere (Verbs Conjugated with Essere)

Infinitive	Singular Past Participle (Masc., Fem.)	Plural Past Participle (Masc., Fem.)	Translation
andare *(to go)*	**andato, andata**	**andati, andate**	*has/have gone, went, did go*
arrivare *(to arrive)*	**arrivato, arrivata**	**arrivati, arrivate**	*has/have arrived, arrived, did arrive*
cadere *(to fall)*	**caduto, caduta**	**caduti, cadute**	*has/have fallen, fell, did fall*
diventare *(to become)*	**diventato, diventata**	**diventati, diventate**	*has/have become, became, did become*
entrare *(to enter)*	**entrato, entrata**	**entrati, entrate**	*has/have entered, entered, did enter*

Infinitive	Singular Past Participle (Masc., Fem.)	Plural Past Participle (Masc., Fem.)	Translation
essere *(to be)*	**stato, stata**	**stati, state**	*has/have been, was, were*
morire *(to die)*	**morto, morta**	**morti, morte**	*has/have died, died, did die*
nascere *(to be born)*	**nato, nata**	**nati, nate**	*was/were born*
partire *(to leave)*	**partito, partita**	**partiti, partite**	*has/have left, left, did leave*
restare *(to stay)*	**restato, restata**	**restati, restate**	*has/have stayed, stayed, did stay*
rimanere *(to stay, to remain)*	**rimasto, rimasta**	**rimasti, rimaste**	*has/have stayed, remained*
(ri)tornare *(to return)* **(tornare** and **ritornare)**	**tornato, tornata**	**tornati, tornate**	*has/have returned, returned, did return*
salire *(to go upstairs, to get on a train or bus, to get in the car)*	**salito, salita**	**saliti, salite**	*has/have gone up, went up, did go up*
scendere *(to go down stairs, to get off of a train or bus, to get out of a car)*	**sceso, scesa**	**scesi, scese**	*has/have gone down, went down, did go down, got off*
stare *(to be, to stay)*	**stato, stata**	**stati, state**	*was, were*
uscire *(to go out)*	**uscito, uscita**	**usciti, uscite**	*has/have gone out, went out, did go out*
venire *(to come)*	**venuto, venuta**	**venuti, venute**	*has/have come, came, did come*

The following shows some very common usages of intransitive verbs, which take **essere:**

>> Verbs in the house of **essere**, starting with the versatile **stare**. **Stare** means either *to stay/to be*, when you refer to whether someone is well or not, such as **stare bene/male** *(to be well/unwell)*. Uniquely, **stare** shares the same past participle with **essere: stato, stata, stati, state** *(stayed/felt)*.

Lucio è stato male. *(Lucio was ill.)*

>> Most verbs of motion, used literally or metaphorically.

Siamo arrivati a Genova. *(We arrived in Genoa.)*

>> Verbs conveying a change of status in the subject, such as **invecchiare** *(to age)*, **nascere** *(to be born)*, **crescere** *(to grow up)*, and **morire** *(to die)*:

Mio padre è nato nel 1963. *(My father was born in 1963.)*

>> All reflexive verbs, such as **svegliarsi** *(to wake up)* and **rompersi** *(to break)* (see Chapter 3 for more on reflexive verbs):

Mi sono svegliato. *(I woke up.)*

Mi sono rotto un dito. *(I broke my finger.)*

Using piacere in the passato prossimo

Because **piacere** *(to like)* is such a common verb, and it also takes **essere** as its helping verb, it deserves its own section in this chapter. You can see how the verb **piacere** works in the present in Chapter 3.

Piacere always agrees with what's being liked.

So, the structure is, frequently:

Indirect object pronoun + **essere** (third person singular or plural) + **piaciuto/a/i/e**

Note the slightly irregular past participle, which agrees in gender and number with what is liked, not with who is doing the liking. Here's an example:

Mi è piaciuta l'opera! *(I liked the opera!)*

Table 6-4 illustrates **piacere** in the present indicative and **passato prossimo**.

TABLE 6-4 Piacere in the Present and the Passato Prossimo

Present Singular and Present Plural	Passato Prossimo Singular and Plural
piace, sing.	
Mi piace la pizza. (*I like pizza.*)	**Mi è piaciuta la pizza.** (*I liked the pizza.*) The past participle **piaciuta** here has to agree with **pizza.**
piacciono, pl.	
Mi piacciono le fragole. (*I like strawberries.*)	**Mi sono piaciute le fragole.** (*I liked the strawberries.*) The verb **piaciute** here agrees with **fragole.**

Using the Passato Prossimo

Being able to know when to use the **passato prossimo** is important when speaking Italian. The following explores the different uses of the **passato prossimo** and examines some phrases commonly used with this tense.

Recognizing when to utilize the passato prossimo

The following list breaks down four principal uses for the **passato prossimo:**

» To describe an action begun and completed in the past (compare this use with the **imperfetto** tense's ongoing and habitual actions in the past):

Ieri siamo andati al cinema. (*We went to the movies yesterday.*)

» To describe an action that interrupts an ongoing action in the past (in this case, the ongoing action is in the **imperfetto**):

Io dormivo quando ho sentito un rumore. (*I was sleeping when I heard a noise.*)

REMEMBER

>> With the adverbs **mai** *(ever/never)*, **già** *(already)*, **ancora** *(yet)*, and **sempre** *(always)* (see Chapters 4 and 5 for more on adverbs).

Always place these adverbs between the auxiliary verb (**essere** or **avere**) and past participle, like in the following examples:

Hai <u>mai</u> provato la zuppa inglese? *(Have you ever tried English trifle?)*

No, <u>non</u> ho <u>mai</u> provato la zuppa inglese. *(No, I've never tried English trifle.)*

Qualifying with expressions of time

You frequently need to qualify what kind of past you're talking about, which could be *two hours ago*, *last week*, *yesterday*, and so on. Table 6-5 illustrates some terms typically used with the **passato prossimo**.

TABLE 6-5 Common Expressions of Time

Expression	Example
ieri *(yesterday)*	**I miei genitori sono tornati ieri da St. Maarten.** *(My parents got back from St. Maarten yesterday.)*
ieri sera *(last night, yesterday evening)*	**Ieri sera abbiamo visto Cinema Paradiso.** *(We saw Cinema Paradiso last night.)*
l'altro ieri *(the day before yesterday)*	**I nonni sono partiti l'altro ieri per il Lago di Como.** *(Our grandparents left for Lago di Como the day before yesterday.)*
fa *(ago)*	**cinque minuti fa** *(five minutes ago)*, **un'ora fa** *(an hour ago)*, **tre mesi fa** *(three months ago)*, **due anni fa** *(two years ago)* **Siamo arrivati cinque minuti fa!** *(We arrived 5 minutes ago!)*
scorso/a/i/e *(last)*	**l'anno scorso** *(last year)*, **la settimana scorsa** *(last week)*, **il mese scorso** *(last month)* **La settimana scorsa siamo andati a Palermo.** *(We went to Palermo last week.)*

Forming Perfect Sentences with the Imperfetto

The **imperfetto** is a very regular tense, even for verbs that are irregular in other tenses. And even with the few verbs that are irregular in the imperfect, what changes is the stem of the verb; the endings are always the same. In the following sections, I show you the endings and then discuss the few irregularities you may encounter.

Recognizing regular verbs in the imperfetto

To form the **imperfetto** tense, you start with the infinitive form of -are, -ere, and -ire verbs (such as, for example, **parlare, mettere, partire**). Take the stem of the infinitives and then add the imperfect endings for these verbs.

Here's a breakdown of the imperfect endings for -are, -ere, and -ire verbs. Say these endings to yourself aloud a few times before moving on. This practice can help you commit the endings to memory.

With an -are verb like **parlare** (to speak, to talk), the stem is **parl-**; the endings are -avo, -avi, -ava, -avamo, -avate, -avano, as the following shows:

parlare *(to speak, to talk)*

io **parlavo**	noi **parlavamo**
tu **parlavi**	voi **parlavate**
lui, lei, Lei **parlava**	loro **parlavano**

La mamma parlava al telefonino mentre io guidavo.
(Mom was talking on her cell phone while I was driving.)

With an **-ere** verb like **vendere** *(to sell)*, the stem is **vend-**; the endings are **-evo, -evi, -eva, -evamo, -evate, -evano,** as shown here:

vendere *(to sell)*

io vend<u>e</u>vo	noi **vendevamo**
tu **vendevi**	voi **vendevate**
lui, lei, Lei **vendeva**	loro **vendevano**

I nonni vendevano l'uva che coltivavano. *(My grandparents would/ used to sell the grapes that they grew.)*

With an **-ire** verb like **capire,** the stem is **cap-**; the endings are **-ivo, -ivi, -iva, -ivamo, -ivate, -ivano,** as shown here:

capire *(to understand)*

io **cap<u>i</u>vo**	noi **capivamo**
tu **capivi**	voi **capivate**
lui, lei, Lei **capiva**	loro **capivano**

Una volta capivo il russo, ma ora non più. *(I used to understand Russian, but not anymore.)*

REMEMBER

The third to last letter of the **imperfetto** endings reflects whether the verb is of the first (**-are**), second (**-ere**), or third conjugation (**-ire**). I underline the characteristic vowel of the verbs in the first person in the preceding verb tables, to drive that point home.

Dealing with a few scoundrels: Irregular verbs

As I say throughout this book, in most cases, you can't really find any criteria for recognizing irregular verbs. I list them for you in the following sections. You just have to learn them by heart, check out the Appendix, or consult a dictionary. The following sections cover irregular verbs in the **imperfetto.**

Essere (to be): Always irregular

The verb **essere** *(to be)* is irregular in all moods and tenses. In the **imperfetto,** it takes a special stem, **er-,** and adds the **imperfetto**

-**are** endings (even though, in the infinitive, it's an -**ere** verb). This verb table shows you its conjugation.

essere *(to be)*

io **ero**	noi **eravamo**
tu **eri**	voi **eravate**
lui/lei/Lei **era**	loro/Loro **erano**

Io ero stanca. (*I was tired.*)

Piacere (to like): Uses the third person

The verb **piacere** *(to like)* is special in every tense. Here I'm only dealing with the third-person singular — **piaceva** — and plural — **piacevano** — of the **imperfetto** in this book. Check out Chapter 3 and the section "Using piacere in the passato prossimo" earlier in this chapter for a more close-up look at this verb's peculiarities. Here's a brief overview of the usage of **piacere** in the **imperfetto** tense:

>> Use **piaceva** if what was liked (or wasn't liked) is singular or expressed by a verb in the infinitive:

   Non mi piaceva il formaggio quando ero piccolo. *(I didn't like cheese when I was little.)*

   Ti piaceva visitare la tua amica Alyssa. *(You used to like to visit your friend Alyssa.)*

>> Use **piacevano** if what was liked is plural:

   Mi piacevano molto i ravioli. *(I used to like ravioli a lot.)*

Verbs that take an expanded stem

Some verbs that you frequently use in Italian have an irregular form in the **imperfetto** tense. With these common verbs, such as **bere, dire, fare,** and **tradurre,** all you have to do is add the regular -**ere** imperfect endings (-**evo, -evi, -eva, -evamo, -evate, -evano**) to the expanded stem (see Table 6-6).

TABLE 6-6 **Verbs with an Expanded Stem**

Infinitive	Expanded Stem for the Imperfetto
bere (to drink)	**bev-**
dire (to say/to tell)	**dic-**
fare (to do/to make)	**fac-**
tradurre (to translate)	**traduc-**

I want to give you one example of a complete conjugation of **tradurre** in the **imperfetto**:

tradurre (to translate)

io **traducevo**	noi **traducevamo**
tu **traducevi**	voi **traducevate**
lui/lei/Lei **traduceva**	loro/Loro **traducevano**

Noi traducevamo Dante. (We were translating Dante./ We used to translate Dante.)

Perfecting the Uses of the Imperfetto

Because the **imperfetto** allows you to talk about things that occurred over an indeterminate period of time in the past, you can use it to express ongoing states, such as feelings, emotions, physical attributes, states of affairs, and habits.

In addition to fairy tales, here are some situations that you can use as guidelines for choosing the **imperfetto** over another past tense (this list isn't exhaustive):

>> Conditions and states of being:

Quando ero bambino ero felice. (When I was a child, I was happy.)

>> Physical descriptions:

Mia sorella era alta e aveva i capelli lunghi. (My sister was tall and had long hair.)

>> Interrupted actions in the past:

Quando suo fratello ha telefonato, Adriana scriveva una lettera. *(When her brother called, Adriana was writing a letter.)*

>> Two ongoing contemporaneous actions in the past. You often see the word **mentre** *(while, during)* in this circumstance:

Ieri sera, Robert guardava la partita mentre Giancarlo giocava con Nico. *(Last night, Robert was watching the game while Giancarlo was playing with Nico.)*

>> Habitual activities in the past:

Quando ero bambino, passavo sempre l'estate in montagna. *(When I was a child, I used to spend/I would always spend the summer in the mountains.)*

>> Age in the past:

Mio padre aveva quindici anni quando è venuto negli Stati Uniti. *(My dad was 15 years old when he came to the United States.)*

>> Desires/wishes in the past [use the verbs **volere** *(to want)*, **desiderare** *(to desire/to wish)*, **sperare** *(to hope)*, **amare** *(to love)*, **piacere** *(to like)*]:

Da piccola volevo/desideravo diventare veterinaria. *(When I was little I wanted to/I wished to become a veterinarian.)*

>> To convey an action in the past that translates as *used to*:

Quando Nicole era giovane, andava ogni weekend a ballare. *(When Nicole was young, she went/used to go/would go dancing every weekend.)*

When the Going Gets Tricky: The Imperfetto and Passato Prossimo

Sometimes, you may find yourself in a situation where you can't figure out whether you're talking about an event that happened and is over or a condition that occurred in the past. You can't always clearly see whether to use the **imperfetto** or **passato prossimo**.

In the following sections, I give you guidelines about

>> Which keywords can trigger a lightbulb when you're trying to figure out which tense to use

>> What the special meanings are for **sapere** *(to know)* and **conoscere** *(to know)*

Grasping key terms

In Italian, you use the **passato prossimo** to talk about situations that began and ended in the past. Here are terms that often trigger the **passato prossimo**:

>> **all'improvviso** *(all of a sudden/suddenly)*

>> **immediatamente** *(immediately)*

>> **quando** *(when)*

>> **quella volta** *(that time)*:

  Di solito andavo alla riunione; quella volta non sono andata. *(I usually went to the meeting; that time, I did not go.)*

>> **ieri; ieri, invece** *(yesterday/yesterday/instead)*

>> **ad un tratto** *(suddenly)*

>> **due ore fa** *(two years ago)*

>> **il mese scorso** *(last month)*

>> **domenic**a *(on Sunday; or any other day of the week)*

>> **una volta** *(once)*

>> **e quindi** *(and so)*

In Italian, you use the **imperfetto** to talk about an ongoing continuous action, age, feelings, among other things. The following grouping gives you some common terms generally associated with the **imperfetto**:

>> **di solito** *(usually)*

>> **sempre** *(always)*

>> **spesso** *(often)*

>> **frequentemente** *(frequently)*

>> **d'estate** *(in the summer; or any other season)*

- » **ogni giorno** *(every day)*
- » **da piccolo/a** *(when I was little)*
- » **quando ero piccolo/a** *(when I was little)*
- » **da bambino/a** *(as a child)*
- » **da giovane** *(as a young person)*
- » **mentre** *(while)*
- » **la domenica, il lunedì, ecc.** *(on Sundays, on Mondays, and so on)*
- » **c'era una volta** *(once upon a time)*

Sometimes you link sentences together using the **passato prossimo** in one and the **imperfetto** in the other. For example: **Guardavo** [imperfetto] **la TV quando è mancata** [passato prossimo] **la luce.** *(I was watching TV when the electricity went out.)*

Differentiating between sapere and conoscere

Sapere *(to know how to do something or to know information about something)* and **conoscere** *(to know or to be acquainted with someone or something)* have different meanings in both the **passato prossimo** and **imperfetto**. Note the following:

- » **Sapere** in the **passato prossimo** means *to learn* or *to find out:*

  Ho saputo che domani c'è sciopero. *(I learned/found out that there's a strike tomorrow.)*
- » **Sapere** in the **imperfetto** means that *you used to know how to do something:*

  Sapevo suonare il violino da piccola. *(I used to know how to play the violin when I was little.)*
- » **Conoscere** in the **passato prossimo** means *to meet someone for the first time:*

  Ieri ho conosciuto la donna della mia vita. *(Last night, I met the woman of my dreams.)*
- » **Conoscere** in the **imperfetto** implies *knowing someone or something in the past:*

  Conoscevo Roma molto bene una volta. *(I used to know Rome very well once upon a time.)*

IN THIS CHAPTER

» **Utilizing the future**

» **Denoting the future with common expressions**

» **Springing forward with regular verbs**

» **Forming irregular stems**

» **Expressing the future in the past**

» **Foretelling, wondering, and predicting with the future**

Chapter **7**

Che Sarà Sarà: Looking to the Future

The future isn't ours to see, hence the phrase that heads this chapter **che sarà, sarà** *(whatever will be, will be)*, from the eponymous song. The future tense is quite common and easy to form. As its name implies, the future is a tense you employ to talk about an event that hasn't yet taken place or something that may take place in the very near and not so very near future.

Italian has two future forms:

» **Futuro semplice** *(simple future)*: **Andrò.** *(I will go.)*

» **Futuro anteriore** *(future perfect)*: **Sarò andato.** *(I will have gone.)*

In this chapter, you cover how to form the future tense, which I will simply call *the future* throughout. You explore how to combine the future with other, more precise phrases that indicate time. In English, to form the future you simply put the words *am going to* or *will* in front of an unconjugated verb, for example, *I'm going to get a new car in May*. Italian verbs, however, have very specific future endings, and the good news is that the endings are all the same for all kinds of verbs — **-are, -ere, -ire,** and the irregular verbs.

TIP

A great way to learn many Italian verb tenses is through songs and poetry that help reinforce the structure while giving you listening (and speaking) practice. Here are a few great songs that employ the future tense. Just look up the songs and the lyrics online:

>> *Diamante lei e luce lui* by Annalisa

>> *Con te partirò* by Andrea Bocelli

>> *Sere nere* by Tiziano Ferro

>> *Io canto* by Laura Pausini

Using the Future

Sometimes in English, you use the present to talk about the future. In Italian, you certainly may also use the present to say something like **Non vado a lavorare domani** *(I'm not going to work tomorrow)*, but the following translations show you that the future is frequently used in Italian (when it translates as the present tense in English):

>> To describe events happening in the future (usually a far or unspecified future):

Un giorno sarò ricco e famoso. *(One day I will be rich and famous.)*

>> To express the intention to do something in the future:

Penso che andrò in California il prossimo anno. *(I think I'll go to California next year.)*

>> To express a possibility or probability:

Hanno bussato alla porta, sarà l'UPS che consegna il pacco. *(Someone knocked on the door; it may be UPS delivering the package.)*

>> When the first verb of a sentence (either a subordinate or main clause) is in the future, often with the terms **quando** *(when)* and **se** *(if)*:

Quando finirai il liceo, andrai all'università. *(When you finish high school, you'll go to college.)*

Se mangerai da noi, ti preparerò le lasagne. *(If you eat at our house, I'll make lasagna for you.)*

>> You use the **futuro anteriore** *(the future prefect)* when a future event precedes another future event. Refer to the

section "Forming the Futuro Anteriore" later in this chapter for how to form it:

Quando tornerai a casa, Ugo sarà già partito. *(By the time you return home, Ugo will have already left.)*

These sections point out some words that help you identify when something is in the future and explain how you can use the present to refer to the future.

Identifying common expressions denoting the future

Like in English, you frequently use Italian words and phrases that translate as, for example, *next* and *in x amount of time*.

Having these expressions in your toolbox helps you to identify that the event is occurring next month or in three years, rather than, for example, yesterday, last week, or two months ago (when you would use the **passato prossimo** or **imperfetto** tenses, which you can find in Chapter 6). Table 7-1 offers some common future tense expressions that come in handy when expressing the future.

TABLE 7-1 Common Terms Denoting the Future

Italian	Translation
prossimo	*next*
l'anno prossimo	*next year*
il mese prossimo	*next month*
fra	*in*
fra 10 anni	*in 10 years*
fra 100 anni	*in 100 years*
domani	*tomorrow*
dopodomani	*day after tomorrow*
se	*if*
quando	*when*
nel futuro	*in the future*
nel 2050 . . .	*in 2050 . . .*

Using the present to talk about the future

All languages have rules, and even basic conjugations can be a challenge at first. Not only do Italian verb forms vary more than they do in English, but Italian also takes a few more liberties in using the present tense to describe the future.

In Italian, you talk about the future by using the present tense in the following cases:

- ≫ To mention an event that will happen soon:

  La vedo domenica. *(I'll see her on Sunday./I'm seeing her on Sunday.)*

- ≫ To announce a decision that's more or less close in time:

  Quest'estate vado alle Maldive. *(This coming summer, I'm going to the Maldives.)*

- ≫ To refer to an event that's part of a timetable:

  Il semestre autunnale inizia il 10 settembre. *(The fall term begins on September 10.)*

- ≫ To give instructions:

  Quando arrivi a San Francisco, va' direttamente a Palo Alto. *(When you get to San Francisco, go straight to Palo Alto.)*

Forming the Simple Future Tense

You form the future tense by adding the future endings to the infinitive stem of the verb (just like the conditional, which you can read about in Chapter 8). The following sections delve into how to create an infinitive stem out of regular infinitives and how to attach the future endings to it. You also get a healthy dose of key spelling exceptions and irregular future stems, so you have everything you need to venture out into the future.

Regular verbs

The simple future tense in Italian is a thing of beauty: You conjugate all verbs — both regular and irregular, ending in — -are, -ere, -ire — in exactly the same way. You just have to memorize one set of endings!

Table 7-2 lists the endings for all three conjugations, followed by a sample conjugation table. All verbs — regular and irregular — place the accent on the same vowels **ò** and **à**. Add stress to these syllables when speaking them (and also in your head when reading them).

TABLE 7-2 ## Simple Future Endings for All Verbs

Person	Verb Endings
io	-ò
tu	-ai
lui/lei/Lei	-à
noi	-emo
voi	-ete
loro/Loro	-anno

Forming an infinitive stem requires knowing where to cut the infinitive. Just follow these steps:

1. **Take the infinitive and cut off the final e.**

However, in **-are** verbs, you have one more step: change the **a** of the infinitive to **e**.

For example:

- **parlare** becomes **parler-**
- **prendere** becomes **prender-**
- **partire** becomes **partir-**

2. **Add the endings: -ò, -ai, -à, -emo, -ete, -anno.**

Check out the following for the future conjugation for an **-are** verb. Verbs ending in **-ere** and **-ire** conjugate the same way.

guardare *(to look at)*	
io **guarderò**	noi **guarderemo**
tu **guarderai**	voi **guarderete**
lui/lei/Lei **guarderà**	loro/Loro **guarderanno**

Massimo non mi guarderà mai. *(Massimo will never look at me.)*

Here are a few more examples of regular verbs in the future tense.

>> **Parleremo con il sindaco del problema.** *(We're going to speak to the mayor about the problem.)*

>> **Il gruppo di amiche leggerà un romanzo di Elsa Morante insieme.** *(The group of friends will read a novel by Elsa Morante together.)*

>> **Gianni e Piero correranno la Maratona di New York.** *(Gianni and Piero will be running the New York Marathon.)*

>> **Lavorerò duro fino a dicembre.** *(I'm going to work hard until December.)*

>> **Daniel, quando partirai per la Croazia?** *(Daniel, when are you leaving for Croatia?)*

Reflexive verbs in the future are conjugated just like all the other regular verbs:

1. **Drop the final e when forming the infinitive stem, after you've removed the si.**

2. **Include the reflexive pronouns (see Chapter 3 for reflexive verbs).**

Here are two examples:

>> **alzarsi** *(to get up)*: **Domani, mi alzerò alle 6.** *(Tomorrow, I'm going to get up at 6.)*

>> **divertirsi** (to have fun/enjoy oneself): **Ci divertiremo quest'estate.** *(We're going to have fun this summer.)*

Stem-changing regular verbs

For verbs that end in –**ciare** and –**giare**, such as **cominciare** (*to begin*) and **mangiare** (*to eat*), drop the i to preserve the soft sound of the infinitive **c** (like in *cherry*) and **g** (like in *Jerry*). Remember to change the **a** to **e** in the stem, as well:

>> **cominciare** becomes **comincer-**

>> **mangiare** becomes **manger-**

>> **studiare** *(to study)* keeps the i in its stem (because it's always pronounced): **studier-**

For verbs that end in -**care** and -**gare**, such as **cercare** *(to look for)* and **pagare** *(to pay)*, place **ch** and **gh** before the endings to preserve the hard sound of the infinitive **c** (as in *cat*) and **g** (as in *gondola*). Since they are -**are** verbs, you also need to change the **a** to **e** in the stem:

>> **pagare** becomes **pagher-**

>> **cercare** becomes **cercher-**

Here are a few more examples of stem-changing future verbs:

>> **Pagheremo noi il conto.** *(We're going to pay the bill.)*

>> **Quando cominceranno le vacanze?** *(When is vacation going to start?)*

>> **Mangerò un gelato appena arriverò a Ravenna.** *(I'm going to have an ice cream as soon as I get to Ravenna.)*

Irregular verbs

You have to consider some irregular-verb issues when dealing with the simple future tense (just like any Italian tense). You do this by transforming the infinitive to irregular future stems; it's still considered an infinitive stem, albeit an irregular infinitive stem. (These are the exact same in the conditional tense that I discuss in Chapter 8, so you only have to learn this set once.) The endings of regular infinitive stems are exactly the same as the endings of regular verbs: -**ò, -ai, -à, -emo, -ete, -anno**.

The following sections walk you through the future of the two most common verbs, **essere** and **avere,** and introduce you to some of the most common and essential irregular infinitive stems that you will need to be proficient in the future tense.

Working with essere and avere

The heading of this chapter (**Che sarà sarà**) is a useful way to always remember the irregular infinitive stem (**sar-**) of the verb **essere** *(to be)*, as follows:

sar- + the regular future ending

The verb **avere** *(to have)* is much less irregular, as you can see here:

avr- + the regular future ending

The following verb tables show their future-tense conjugations.

essere *(to be)*

io **sarò**	noi **saremo**
tu **sarai**	voi **sarete**
lui/lei/Lei **sarà**	loro/Loro **saranno**

Dove sarai tra vent'anni? *(Where will you be in 20 years?)*
Sarete alla casa di Annika? *(Will you all be at Annika's house?)*

avere *(to have)*

io **avrò**	noi **avremo**
tu **avrai**	voi **avrete**
lui/lei/Lei **avrà**	loro/Loro **avranno**

Guarda quei ragazzi: avranno vent'anni al massimo.
(Look at those guys: They can't be older than 20.)

Se avremo tempo, ci fermeremo anche a Padova.
(If we have time, we'll also stop in Padua.)

Looking at dare, fare, and stare

What makes the verbs **dare** *(to give)*, **fare** *(to do/to make)*, and **stare** *(to be/to stay)* irregular is that the **a** doesn't change to an **e,** unlike all the other regular **-are** verbs in the future tense:

» **dare** *(to give)* becomes **dar-**

   Daremo una festa per Amalia. *(We're going to have a party for Amalia.)*

» **fare** becomes **far-**

   Cosa farai da grande? *(What are you going to be when you grow up?)*

   Sarò medico. *(I'm going to be a doctor.)*

> » **stare** becomes **star-**
>
> **Giulia e Violetta staranno a casa stasera.** *(Giulia and Violetta are staying home tonight.)*

Figuring out stem-changing irregular verbs

Using other stem-changing irregular verbs in the future tense is easy-peasy. Just add the future endings (-**ò**, -**ai**, -**à**, -**emo**, -**ete**, -**anno**) to these irregular stems, and you're good to go.

Some of these future stems follow a pattern: Remove the final vowel and the second-to-last vowel forms the infinitive, whereas other verbs double up on the **r**. Noticing these patterns in the following list can help you to group them and remember them:

- » **andare** *(to go)*: **andr-** + future ending
- » **bere** *(to drink)*: **berr-** + future ending
- » **cadere** *(to fall)*: **cadr-** + future ending
- » **dovere** *(to have to/must)*: **dovr-** + future ending
- » **potere** *(must/shall/be able to)*: **potr-** + future ending
- » **rimanere** *(to remain/to stay)*: **rimarr-** + future ending
- » **sapere** *(to know how to)*: **sapr-** + future ending
- » **vedere** *(to see)*: **vedr-** + future ending
- » **venire** *(to come)*: **verr-** + future ending
- » **vivere** *(to live)*: **vivr-** + future ending
- » **volere** *(to want)*: **vorr-** + future ending

Here are just a few examples that use the irregular stems:

- » **Dovremo ridare questo esame.** *(We'll have to take this exam again.)*
- » **Non so quando andrò a Indianapolis.** *(I don't know when I'll be going to Indianapolis.)*
- » **Non saprò mai sciare come te.** *(I'll never know how to ski like you.)*
- » **Vorranno conoscerti, prima o poi.** *(They'd like to meet you, sooner or later.)*

>> **State attenti, rimarrete senza benzina!** *(Be careful, you'll run out of gas!)*

>> **Jesse vedrà Liborio ad Amalfi.** *(Jesse is going to see Liborio in Amalfi.)*

>> **Potrai fermarti a Venezia per qualche giorno.** *(You can stop off in Venice for a few days.)*

>> **Che cosa berranno gli ospiti?** *(What will the guests drink?)*

>> **Voi vorrete andare alla partita quando sarete a Milano?** *(Do you all want to go to the game when you're in Milan?)*

Forming the Futuro Anteriore

The **futuro anteriore** (or future perfect) is a compound tense that describes a future event happening before another future event. Compound tense means that it's comprised of forming these two parts together:

>> The simple future of the auxiliary (or helping) verb **essere** *(to be)* or **avere** *(to have)*

>> The past participle of the verb

Refer to the section "Working with **essere** and **avere**" earlier in this chapter, where I explain how to form the future tense of **essere** and **avere**. Chapter 6, in the context of the **passato prossimo** tense *(present perfect)*, shows you how to determine which auxiliary verb to choose and how to form the past participle.

The following verb tables give you the future perfect of **mangiare** *(to eat)*, which uses **avere,** and **tornare** *(to return/to go back)*, which uses **essere.**

mangiare *(to eat)*	
io **avrò mangiato**	noi **avremo mangiato**
tu **avrai mangiato**	voi **avrete mangiato**
lui/lei/Lei **avrà mangiato**	loro/Loro **avranno mangiato**

Avremo già mangiato quando Nicola arriverà.
(We'll already have eaten by the time Nicola arrives.)

tornare *(to return, to go back)*

io **sarò tornato/tornata**	noi **saremo tornati/tornate**
tu **sarai tornato/tornata**	voi **sarete tornati/tornate**
lui/lei/Lei **sarà tornato/tornata**	loro/Loro **saranno tornati/ tornate**

Fra 20 anni saremo tornati in Italia varie volte.
(In twenty years, we'll have gone back to Italy several times.)

Pensate, fra 2 giorni saremo già arrivati in Sicilia.
(Just think, in two days we'll have already arrived in Sicily.)

To understand how to use the future perfect, compare the verb tenses in the following example sentences:

» Present: **Quando arriva in ufficio, gli telefono.**
(I call him when he gets to the office.)

» Future: **Quando arriverà in ufficio, gli telefonerò.**
(I will call him when he gets to the office.)

» Future perfect: **Quando sarà arrivato in ufficio, gli telefonerò.** *(When he's arrived at the office, I'll call him.)*

Predicting with the Future

Sometimes you use the simple future and the **futuro anteriore** to express probability and possibility, and to say maybe and perhaps. This is called the **futuro di probabilità.** Whether you're projecting probability depends on context. You just can't tell sometimes.

If I say, **Il cane mangerà il cibo del gatto,** it could mean either *The dog is going to eat the cat's food,* or *The dog is probably going to eat the cat's food.*

Here are a couple illustrative examples of the simple **futuro di probabilità:**

» **Chi è alla porta?** *(Who's at the door?)*
Sarà il postino. *(It's probably the letter carrier.)*

>> **Che ore sono?** *(What time is it?)*

Saranno le cinque. *(It's probably five o'clock.)*

>> **Il professore avrà settanta anni.** *(The professor is probably or must be 70 years old.)*

And here are a couple of illustrative examples of the future perfect **futuro di probabilità:**

>> **Dove sono i ragazzi?** *(Where are the kids?)*

Boh! Avranno perso il treno! *(I don't know, they've probably missed the train!)*

>> **Il gatto avrà mangiato la bistecca.** *(The cat probably ate the steak.)*

>> **Sarà tornato in ufficio.** *(He must have gone back to work/to the office.)*

Chapter **8**

Using Verb Moods

A verb's *mood* reflects an attitude, intent, and reality. Italian moods come in four inflections:

» **Indicative mood:** The most commonly used, it states a fact and a certainty and expresses several tenses. This book covers the present indicative (see Chapter 3), the **passato prossimo** *(present perfect)*, **imperfetto** *(imperfect)* (refer to Chapter 6), and the future (see Chapter 7). There's also the **trapassato prossimo** *(pluperfect indicative)*, which I don't cover in this book.

» **Imperative mood:** This mood covers the commands.

» **Subjunctive mood:** This mood reflects wishing, feeling, and doubt (among other things). It has its own tenses, which include the present subjunctive, the past subjunctive, the imperfect subjunctive, and the pluperfect subjunctive. This chapter covers two of those four.

» **Conditional:** This expresses what would or could happen; I like to call it the polite tense, although it has many more uses than being nice. There are two conditional tenses, the present conditional and the past conditional. Some linguists say the conditional is both a tense and a mood.

This chapter focuses on the imperative, subjunctive, and conditional.

Giving Commands with the Imperative Mood

You use the imperative when addressing a person directly, such as **Stai attenta!** *(Be careful!)*. The imperative is the mood of commands and exhortations, such as **Abbi fiducia!** *(Have faith!)*. The imperative in Italian always implies a direct command, and you mainly use it in conversation. A sentence such as **Andiamo! È tardi!** *(Let's go! It's late!)* lies between order and suggestion (more of an urging than a command).

REMEMBER

In Italian, there are four ways of saying you. The imperative is employed mostly (but not exclusively) in the second-person singular (**tu**) and plural (**voi**). The following sections explore the important things you need to know about the imperative.

Forming the imperative

Knowing how to form the imperative in all its persons is important so you can issue affirmative and negative commands. This chapter also covers what to do with pronouns, as in the command **Svegliati!** *(Wake up!)*.

Staying informal with the imperative form of regular verbs

The informal imperative form addresses people with whom you are familiar or when the degree of formality is low. Table 8-1 shows the different conjugations for informal usage (**tu, noi,** and **voi** persons) of imperatives.

The informal imperative forms of **tu, noi,** and **voi** are identical to the corresponding present tense forms, with one exception: In the **tu** form of **-are** verbs, the **-i** becomes **-a**.

WARNING

Sometimes, the only difference between the imperative and the indicative is your tone of voice. Always include an exclamation point when writing or speaking in the imperative. Refer to Chapter 3 on the present indicative tense if you need a refresher. Imagine how different these two sentences sound:

> **Guardate la partita.** *(You're watching the game.)*
>
> **Guardate la partita!** *(Watch the game!)*

TABLE 8-1 **Informal Imperatives of Regular Verbs**

Verb	Informal Singular	Informal Plural
guardare *(to look, to watch)*	**(tu) guarda!** *([you] look/ watch!)*	**(noi) guardiamo!** *(let's look/ watch!)*
		(voi) guardate! *([you] look/ watch!)*
prendere *(to take/ have/get)*	**(tu) prendi!** *([you] take/ have/get!)*	**(noi) prendiamo!** *(let's take/ have/get!)*
		(voi) prendete! *([you] take/ have/get!)*
dormire *(to sleep)*	**(tu) dormi!** *([you] sleep!)*	**(noi) dormiamo!** *(let's sleep!)*
		(voi) dormite! *([you] sleep!)*
finire *(to finish)*	**(tu) finisci!** *([you] finish!)*	**(noi) finiamo!** *(let's finish!)*
		(voi) finite! *([you] finish!)*

Forming the formal imperative

The formal imperative (**Lei/Loro**) is used less frequently than the informal command form, but you must use it in certain situations where a certain degree of formality is required, such as when entering a store, interacting with wait-staff, your own boss, or talking to older people (such as your professors and your friends' parents).

REMEMBER

After you figure out how to conjugate **Lei** and **Loro** in the imperative, you can also conjugate verbs in the present subjunctive because the forms are identical.

Everyday spoken Italian mostly uses the informal imperative form of **voi** when speaking to a group:

> **Signore e signori, ascoltate con attenzione!** *(Ladies and gentlemen, listen carefully!)*

When you form the formal imperative in Italian, you have a sort of reverse rule for the **tu** and **Lei** forms — the **-are** conjugations are a flip of the **-ere** and **-ire** conjugations. Table 8-2 spells this out a little more clearly.

TIP

To construct a formal imperative, drop the -**are**, -**ere**, -**ire** from the stem and add the formal imperative endings. -**Are** verbs take -**i/ino** endings and -**ere/-ire** verbs take -**a/ano** endings (see Table 8-2 for some examples).

TABLE 8-2 Formal Imperatives of Regular Verbs

Verb	Formal Singular	Formal Plural
guardare *(to look)*	**(Lei) guardi!** *([you] look!)*	**(Loro) guardino!** *([you] look!)*
prendere *(to take)*	**(Lei) prenda!** *([you] take!)*	**(Loro) prendano!** *([you] take!)*
dormire *(to sleep)*	**(Lei) dorma!** *([you] sleep!)*	**(Loro) dormano!** *([you] sleep!)*
finire *(to finish)*	**(Lei) finisca!** *([you] finish!)*	**(Loro) finiscano!** *([you] finish!)*

Tackling irregular verbs

Some Italian verbs have an irregular conjugation in the imperative. The following section walks you through the conjugations of some of these verbs.

The verbs **andare** *(to go)*, **dare** *(to give)*, **fare** *(to do, to make)*, and **stare** *(to stay)* have both regular and irregular **tu** informal imperatives: **va'/vai, fa'/fai, da'/dai,** and **sta'/stai. Sta' zitto e fa' quel che dico!** *(Be quiet, and do as I say!).*

The verb **dire** *(to say)* is irregular in most forms, as in **Di' la verità!** *(Tell the truth!):* The other persons are **dica!, dite!, diciamo!,** and **dicano!**

REMEMBER

When you walk into a store, or when a server comes to take your order, you frequently hear, **"Dimmi!"** (informal) or **"Mi dica!"** or **"Dica pure!"** (formal). On these occasions, this usage means *"How can I help you?"* — not *"Say it!"/"Tell me!"*

TIP

The best way to construct a formal imperative of irregular verbs is to start with the infinitive. First, conjugate these verbs in the **io** person in the present tense, and then add -**a** and -**ano** to form the formal imperative.

Here's one example of **andare** *(to go/to leave)*:

> **Vado.** (**io**, present) *(I'm leaving.)*
>
> **Vada!** (**Lei**, imperative) *(Leave!)*
>
> **Vadano!** (**Loro**, imperative) *(Leave!)*

The verbs **avere** *(to have)* and **essere** *(to be)* are irregular (among many other verbs). Check the Appendix for their conjugations.

You can tone down the imperious effect of the imperative by adding the word **pure** *(by all means/please)* after the command. You can also throw in **prego** *(please/by all means)*:

> **Venga pure!** *(By all means, please come!)*
>
> **Prego, mi segua!** *(Please, follow me!)*

TIP

Sometimes, you may hear someone say, **Dai!** The word **Dai!** doesn't necessarily mean *"Give!"* **Dai!** can also mean *Come on!* **Dai! È tardi!** *(Come on! It's late!)*

Examining negative commands

All verbs that have an affirmative command also have a negative command. All of the negative imperative forms — except for the **tu** form — are the exact same in the negative as they are in the affirmative.

You form the negative imperative for **tu** by using the infinitive form of the verb preceded by **non** *(don't)*. This is exclusively for the negative **tu** command:

> **Non finire tutta la torta!** *(Don't finish the whole cake!)*

All of the other negative imperative commands are the exact same form as the affirmative commands: all you do is throw a **non** in front of them.

Adding pronouns to commands

Pronouns are important parts of speech in Italian and are frequently used with commands. Chapter 2 addresses the direct and indirect object pronouns, and Chapter 3 touches on reflexive pronouns.

Pronouns are *always* attached to the command forms **tu, noi,** and **voi,** but they *always* precede the command forms **Lei** and **Loro.**

Here's an example that substitutes a direct object with its pronoun in the **tu** command:

> **Mangia la pasta! Mangiala!** *(Eat the pasta! Eat it!)*

La pasta is a feminine singular direct object: **la** replaces it.

And the same exact sentence using the **Lei** command:

> **Mangi la pasta! La mangi!** *(Eat the pasta! Eat it!)*

With negative informal commands, however, the pronoun may precede or follow the command. If it's the negative **tu,** you should drop the final **-e** when attaching it to the infinitive — it's up to you:

> **Non toccare quella torta! Non la toccare/Non toccarla!**
> *(Don't touch that cake! Don't touch it!)*

You might need to tell someone to leave you alone — or to just leave. Here are two different ways to get rid of them, using the **tu** imperative (with and without a direct object pronoun):

> **Lasciami in pace!** *(Leave me alone!)*

> **Vai/Va' via!** *(Go away!)*

Working with the reflexives

Like the other pronouns, when using a reflexive verb with the affirmative informal commands, the pronoun follows and is attached to the imperative. With the negative **tu, noi,** and **voi** forms, the pronoun may precede or follow:

> **Alzati e lavati!** *(Get up and get washed!)*

> **Non preoccuparti!/Non ti preoccupare!** *(Don't worry!)*

Refer to Table 8-3 for the use of reflexive pronouns with the imperative mood.

TABLE 8-3 **Reflexive Imperatives**

Affirmative Commands	Translation	Negative Commands	Translation
Vestiti!	*Get dressed!* (Literally: *Dress yourself!*)	**Non ti vestire così!/ Non vestirti così!**	*Don't dress like that!*
Si vesta! (Lei)	*Get dressed!* (Literally: *Dress yourself!*)	**Non si vesta ancora!**	*Don't get dressed yet!* (Let's say you're at the doctor's office.)
Vestiamoci!	*Let's get dressed!*	**Non vestiamoci!/ Non ci vestiamo!**	*Let's not get dressed!*
Vestitevi!	*Get dressed!*	**Non vestitevi!/Non vi vestite!**	*Don't get dressed!*
Si vestano! (Loro)	*Get dressed!*	**Non si vestano!**	*Don't get dressed!*

When you issue a negative command in the formal imperative, you always place the pronoun between **non** and the imperative:

TIP

Non si preoccupi, signora! *(Don't worry, Ma'am!)*

Focusing on the Subjunctive Mood

The subjunctive mood exists in English too — for example, you say "It's important that she understand this" — the present subjunctive. In some Romance languages, such as French, the subjunctive is being used less and less. In Italian, however, the subjunctive is used much more often, especially to express doubt, feelings, wishes, and uncertainty.

In this section, I introduce you to the **congiuntivo presente** *(present subjunctive)*. You find out how to form the present subjunctive, work with spelling exceptions and irregular forms, and make the subjunctive a valuable tool in your Italian arsenal. I also very briefly cover the past subjunctive, a compound tense (made up of two parts).

For lack of space, I don't include the imperfect subjunctive, which is commonly used in Italy in hypothetical sentences, as well as other specific circumstances: **Se io fossi te, non lo farei.** *(If I were you, I wouldn't do it.)* I also skip over the pluperfect subjunctive.

Forming the present subjunctive

The formation of the present subjunctive usually calls for a dependent clause, which you frequently introduce with the word **che** *(that)*. Notice the position of the subjunctive in the following sentence and what kind of verb I use in the main clause:

Credo che Emilia dorma poco. *(I think that Emilia sleeps little.)*

In this sentence, **credo** is in the present indicative tense, and **dorma** is in the present subjunctive tense. Note, also, that the subject in the main clause (**io** *[I]*) is different from the subject in the dependent clause (Emilia).

TIP

In English, when I say *I think Emilia sleeps little,* I omit the *that,* but you never omit it in Italian (hence the **che**).

REMEMBER

The personal pronoun is often superfluous and unnecessary in most Italian verb tenses because the person is inherent in the verb form. But in the present subjunctive, you use the same verb form for the first three persons. Therefore, you should use the personal pronoun (**io, tu, lui/lei/Lei**) with the present subjunctive to avoid confusing your reader/listener:

È essenziale che io capisca questo congiuntivo. *(It's essential that I understand this subjunctive.)*

È bene che lei capisca sua nipote. *(It's a good thing that she understands her niece.)*

Check out the Appendix for **parlare** *(to speak)* conjugated in the present subjunctive. Note that the first three persons are the same! **-i, -iamo, -iate,** and **-ino.**

The present subjunctive endings are the same for **-ere** and **-ire** verbs: **-a, -iamo, -iate,** and **-ano.** Refer to the Appendix for **vendere** *(to sell)* and **partire** *(to leave, to depart).*

The endings for **-ire (isc)** verbs in the present subjunctive are **-isca, -iamo, -iate,** and **-iscano.** Check out **capire** *(to understand)* in the Appendix.

REMEMBER

You conjugate reflexive verbs, such as **divertirsi,** just as you do any of the previous **-are, -ere, -ire,** and **-ire (isc)** verbs in the present subjunctive. The only difference is that you need to add the reflexive pronouns. (For more on reflexive verbs and pronouns, see Chapter 3.)

Mastering spelling exceptions and irregular forms

As with the indicative mood, the present subjunctive mood features verbs that undergo spelling changes and irregular verbs. Spelling exceptions are very common, but irregular verbs become easy to handle after you learn their stems and structures.

Some stem-changing considerations: -care, -gare, -ciare, and -giare verbs

One spelling exception calls for you to add an **h** to the end of the stems of **-care** and **-gare** verbs — such as **dimenticare** *(to forget)* and **pagare** *(to pay)* — before you add their subjunctive endings. Doing so allows you to keep the hard "c" and "g" sounds throughout. For example:

> **È probabile che io dimentichi questo congiuntivo.** *(It's likely that I'm going to forget this subjunctive.)*

> **È bene che Pietro paghi la cena.** *(It's good that Pietro's paying for dinner.)*

Other verbs in the present subjunctive, like **cominciare** *(to begin)*, **mangiare** *(to eat)*, **lasciare** *(to leave)*, and **svegliare** *(to wake)* — in other words, verbs that end in **-iare.** Drop their **-i** before you add the subjunctive endings. Use the following verb table for a conjugation of **-iare** verbs.

cominciare *(to begin)*

che io cominci	che noi cominc**iamo**
che tu cominci	che voi cominc**iate**
che lu, lei, Lei cominci	che loro cominc**ino**

È ora che io cominci a studiare. *(It's time that I begin to study.)*

REMEMBER

The three singular forms of each verb are the same, meaning that **io, tu, lui/lei/Lei** are all included in the first conjugation you see.

Recognizing common forms of irregular present subjunctive

Having a handy list of some of the most common forms of the irregular present subjunctive can be helpful. This list isn't exhaustive.

TIP

The conjugations of the **lei** and **loro** imperative (command) forms in the preceding section are essentially the same as the present subjunctive. I put many irregular forms in Table 8-4. (See the Appendix for more.)

TABLE 8-4 ## Some Irregular Present Tense Subjunctive Verbs

Infinitive	Conjugation	Example
avere *(to have)*	abbia, abbiamo, abbiate, abbiano	**Non so chi abbia il mio libro.** *(I don't know who has my book.)*
andare *(to go)*	vada, andiamo, andiate, vadano	**È bene che vadano via.** *(It's a good thing that they're going away.)*
dare *(to give)*	dia, diamo, diate, diano	**Vuoi che gli dia una mano?** *(Do you want for me to give him a hand?)*
dire *(to say)*	dica, diciamo, diciate, dicano	**Sembra che dicano la verità.** *(It seems like they're telling the truth.)*
essere *(to be)*	sia, siamo, siate, siano	**Voglio che tu sia felice.** *(I want for you to be happy.)*
fare *(to do, to make)*	faccia, facciamo, facciate, facciano	**È ora che io faccia il footing.** *(It's time that I begin jogging./It's time for me to go jogging.)*
potere *(to be able to)*	possa, possiamo, possiate, possano	**È strano che i miei amici possano stare fuori fino alle 3 di notte, e io no.** *(It's strange that my friends can stay out until 3 in the morning, and I can't.)*
sapere *(to know)*	sappia, sappiamo, sappiate, sappiano	**Bisogna che tu sappia.** *(You need to know.)*
stare *(to be)*	stia, stiamo, stiate, stiano	**Immagino che stiano ancora insieme.** *(I guess they're still together.)*

Infinitive	Conjugation	Example
uscire *(to go out)*	esca, usciamo, usciate, escano	**Non voglio che tu esca senza il cappotto.** *(I don't want for you to go out without a coat.)*
venire *(to come)*	venga, veniamo, veniate, vengano	**Può darsi che veniamo in Italia.** *(It's possible that we're coming to Italy.)*
volere *(to want)*	voglia, vogliamo, vogliate, vogliano	**Spero che Emilia voglia andare alla spiaggia oggi.** *(I hope that Emilia wants to go to the beach today.)*

Eyeing verbs and expressions that require the subjunctive

The verbs in Table 8-5 all require that their accompanying verbs be in the subjunctive, because they express desires, wishes, commands, emotions, doubts, or disbeliefs. These verbs are the triggers in the main or independent clause; all these expressions should be followed by **che.**

TABLE 8-5 Verbs That Require the Subjunctive

Verb or Expression	Meaning	Verb or Expression	Meaning
augurarsi	*to hope*	non essere certo/a/i/e	*to not be certain*
avere l'impressione	*to have the impression, the/a feeling, the idea*	non essere sicuro/a/i/e	*to not be sure*
avere paura	*to be afraid*	non sapere	*to not know*
chiedere	*to ask for*	pensare	*to think*
credere	*to believe, to think*	permettere	*to allow, to permit*
desiderare	*to desire*	preferire	*to prefer*
dispiacere	*to be sorry*	pretendere	*to demand, to expect*
essere contenta/o/i/e	*to be happy*	sperare	*to hope*
essere triste/i	*to be sad*	volere	*to want*

Here's an example:

Spero che mi telefonino oggi. *(I hope that they call me today.)*

WARNING

Sapere *(to know)* takes the indicative in a subordinate clause, and **non sapere** *(to not know)* takes the subjunctive. For example, compare:

So che lei è onesta. *(I know she is honest.)* The **è** is in the indicative.

Non so che lei sia onesta. *(I don't know if/that she's honest.)* The **sia** is in the subjunctive.

Noting impersonal expressions with and without subjunctive

Another instance when you frequently should use the subjunctive is when a verb in the main clause is an *impersonal expression* and the subject of the dependent clause is articulated, such as in the following samples:

È importante studiare. *(It's important to study.)* In this example, no subject is expressed.

È importante che io studi. *(It's important that I study.)* In this example, the subject in the dependent clause is specified, so you use the subjunctive.

An impersonal expression has no specific subject (hence the nominative *impersonal*) and often translates as *one, you,* or *it.* These impersonal expressions usually start with the third-person singular of *the verb essere (to be): È bene che . . .* (*It's a good thing that . . .).* Table 8-6 provides you with a list of common impersonal expressions that require the subjunctive.

TIP

Not all impersonal expressions, however, require the subjunctive. For example, the impersonal expressions **È certo che** . . . *(It's certain that . . .)* and **È sicuro che** . . . *(It's a sure thing that . . .)* express a certainty. Therefore, the clause to follow needs to be in the indicative and not the subjunctive: **È certo che lui viene.** *(It's certain that he's going to come.)*

TABLE 8-6 **Impersonal Expressions That Take the Subjunctive**

Expression	Meaning
è essenziale che	È essenziale che lo **facciate**. (*It's essential that you* [pl.] *do it.*)
bisogna che	*it's necessary that/you have to/one should*
è bene che	*it's good that*
è importante che	*it's important that*
è incredibile che	*it's incredible that*
è inutile che	*it's useless that, it's pointless that*
è male che	*it's bad that*
è meglio che	*it's better that*
è ora che	*it's time that*
è (im)possibile che	*it's (im)possible that*
è (im)probabile che	*it's (im)probable that, it's (un)likely that*
è strano che	*it's strange that*
è triste che	*it's sad that*
pare che	*it seems that*
peccato che	*it's too bad that*
sembra che	*it seems that*

Dabbling with the past subjunctive

The *past subjunctive* is a compound tense, meaning that it always has two parts:

Present subjunctive of either **essere** or **avere** + Past participle

You use the past subjunctive in the dependent (or subordinate) clause if the action in that clause happened before the action in the main or independent clause. For example, you might want to say something like *I don't know if they've arrived*, or *It's strange that they didn't call,* and in those circumstances, you need the past subjunctive in the dependent clause. See Chapter 6 for everything you need on compound tenses **(passato prossimo)** and past participles.

Consider these two examples of forming the past subjunctive. The first example shows a transitive verb — **dormire** *(to sleep)*, which takes **avere** as its helping verb. The second example shows an intransitive verb — **andare** *(to go)*, which takes **essere** as its helping verb:

> **Credo che Nico abbia giocato molto.** *(I think that Nico played a lot.)*

> **Non so se Serena sia andata al parco.** *(I don't know if Serena went to the park.)*

Forming and Using the Conditional

What would you do if you had a million dollars? Where would you have gone on vacation? You might use the conditional mood to deal with such questions.

The conditional mood has a present and past tense:

» **Present conditional:** When you're talking about something that someone would like or is wishing right now

La Signora Rossi ti vorrebbe parlare. *(Mrs. Rossi would like to speak with you.)*

» **Past conditional:** Conveys that something would have been desirable or appropriate, even though it might be too late now to do anything about it

Avrei visto volentieri quel film una seconda volta. *(I would have gladly seen that film a second time.)*

The following sections show you how to form and use the conditional in Italian.

Shaping verbs into the present conditional

The present conditional is a polite tense. It's also used to add politeness to offers, advice, and requests that would otherwise sound too blunt. The present conditional is a simple tense that you form by adding suffixes to the infinitive stem of the verb, and shares the *exact same stem* as the future tense (see Chapter 7 for more about how to form the regular and irregular infinitive stems).

TIP

The conditional is frequently used with words such as **ma** (*but*):

> **Mangerei, ma non ho fame.** *(I would eat, but I'm not hungry.)*

The following sections walk you through how to conjugate regular and irregular verbs in the present conditional tense.

Conjugating regular verbs

The conjugations for regular and irregular verbs in the present conditional are awesomely simple: They have only one set of endings. Just follow this formula:

    Infinitive stem + Conditional ending

These regular infinitive stems of **–are, –ere,** and **–ire** verbs are as follows:

>> **parlare** becomes **parler-** (the **a** in -are verbs turns into an **e**).

   Parlerei con tuo padre. *(I would talk to your dad.)*

>> **mettere** becomes **metter-.**

   Gix metterebbe il divano là. *(Gix would put the couch there.)*

>> **partire** becomes **partir-.**

   Partiremmo subito, ma i ragazzi non sono ancora arrivati. *(We'd leave right away, but the kids haven't arrived yet.)*

The present conditional endings are the same for the three conjugations (-**are**, -**ere**, and -**ire** verbs): -**ei**, -**esti**, -**ebbe**, -**emmo**, -**este**, and -**ebbero**.

Verbs that end in -**ciare** and -**giare**, such as **cominciare** *(to begin)* and **mangiare** *(to eat)*, drop the **i** before the endings to preserve the soft sounds (ch) (as in *chips*) and (gee) (as in *gee whiz!*). Verbs that end in -**care** and -**gare**, such as **cercare** *(to look for)* and **pagare** *(to pay)*, add an **h** to the stem before adding the conditional endings to preserve the hard sound of the infinitive, as in the *c* as in *cat*, and *g* as in *get*.

Piacere *(to like)* is always unique across the tenses. In this book, you're concerned with **piacere** only in the third-person singular (if what you like is singular or an infinitive) or the third-person plural (if what you like is plural). See Chapters 3 and 6 for more on **piacere** (in the present tense and past tenses).

Consider the following examples of **piacere** in the present conditional:

>> With an infinitive: **Mi piacerebbe visitare le Isole Egadi un giorno.** *(I'd like to visit the Egadi Islands one day.)*

>> With something singular: **Mi piacerebbe una pizza.** *(I'd like a pizza.)*

>> With something plural: **Ti piacerebbero le zucchine o le melanzane alla griglia?** *(Would you like zucchini or eggplant on the grill?)*

Piacere in the conditional present is very similar to **volere** *(to want)* in the conditional — both mean *would like*.

Tackling irregular stems

All verbs that have an irregular future stem use the same stem for the conditional. Technically, the conditional does follow a regular pattern — you form it by adding the appropriate endings to the regular and irregular infinitive stems of the verb (see Chapter 7).

You can use **essere** *(to be)* and **avere** *(to have)* by themselves or as auxiliaries in compound tenses. In the present conditional, the stems are the same as for the future tense:

>> **essere** becomes **sar-**

>> **avere** becomes **avr-** (you drop both **e**'s from the infinitive)

Refer to the Appendix to see how **essere** *(to be)* and **avere** *(to have)* are conjugated in the conditional.

When you need to communicate with a moderated tone, you can use the conditional of the verbs **dovere** *(must/shall/ought/need to)*, **potere** *(can/may/to be able to)*, **volere** *(to want to)*, and **sapere** (to know how to) to soften the impact of requests and demands.

If you want something, you can be very assertive and, say (as a child might), **Voglio un gelato!** *(I want ice cream!)*. If you're talking to yourself, this sort of statement is okay, but you may want to be a tad less aggressive and say **Vorrei un gelato!** *(I'd like an ice cream!)*.

Here are a couple songs that provide several examples of the conditional mood. Download the lyrics and Google the song itself so that you can listen and sing along:

>> **"Il mondo che vorrei"** by Laura Pausini

>> **"Io vorrei"** by Lucio Battisti

It's over now! Forming the past conditional

The past conditional expresses the idea that it's too late now and also describes an action that can't occur in the future, either. For example:

Avresti dovuto dirmi! *(You should have told me!)*

Mi sarebbe piaciuto venire alla festa! *(I would have liked to come to the party!)*

To provide more context, compare these two sentences, the first in the present conditional and the second in the past conditional:

Cosa faresti al mio posto? *(What would you do in my situation?)*

Cosa avresti fatto al mio posto? *(What would you have done in my situation?)*

The past conditional is a compound tense (made up of two parts) with the following formula:

Present conditional of **essere** *(to be)* or **avere** *(to have)* + Past participle of the verb

The auxiliary you use depends on which main verb you're using. (Chapter 6 shows you how to decide which auxiliary verb to use.)

Chapter 9

Ten Frequently Mixed-Up Italian Verbs and Phrases

This chapter is a mix of grammar and vocabulary tips intended to help you avoid some simple mistakes and enrich your Italian communicative skills. I start with some verbs and phrases that are considered *false friends* (they are *not* cognates) — words that look similar in Italian and English yet have different meanings. I also offer you some sophisticated expressions that can help you sound like a real Italian — most are idiomatic expressions, meaning that you don't translate them word for word. You're getting a few extra phrases in this chapter, but it's in the spirit of illustrating nuances.

Fare Domanda versus Fare una Domanda

Fare domanda means *to apply* (as in, to a university or for a job), and **fare una domanda** means *to ask a question:*

Faccio domanda per quel lavoro. *(I'm applying for that job.)*

Scusi professore, posso fare una domanda? *(Excuse me professor, may I ask a question?)*

The noun **la domanda** *(question)* comes from the verb **domandare** *(to ask)*.

Giocare versus Suonare

The difference in the meaning of the verbs **giocare** and **suonare** is connotative. **Giocare** means *to play a sport, cards, or chess,* and **suonare** means *to play an instrument.* **Giocare** is a **-care** verb (see Chapter 3 for info on what this means). Here's an example of each:

> **Giochiamo a calcio, e suoniamo il pianoforte.** *(We play soccer, and we play the piano.)*

Lavorare versus Funzionare

Both **lavorare** and **funzionare** mean *to work,* but **lavorare** refers to a person and **funzionare** refers to a mechanical object:

> **Marco lavora oggi fino a tardi, anche se non funziona il suo computer.** *(Marco is working until late today, even though his computer isn't working.)*

Andare in Bagno versus Fare il Bagno

Andare in bagno means *to go to the bathroom,* and **fare il bagno** means *to take a bath* and *to go for a swim.* Here are a few examples that show these verbs in action:

> **Posso andare in bagno?** *(May I go to the bathroom?)*
>
> **Ha fatto il bagno la bambina?** *(Did the baby have a bath?)*
>
> **Non fate il bagno?** *(Aren't you guys going for a swim?)*

Divertirsi versus . . .

Only one verb here. **Divertirsi** has a few meanings: *to have a good time, to enjoy oneself,* and *to have fun.* But no matter how much I talk about this verb, many of my students just don't put it to use. Here's the correct way to express your happiness:

> **Quanto ci siamo divertiti!** *(We had such a good time!/We had so much fun!)*
>
> **Daniel si diverte a sciare con i suoi amici.** *(Daniel has a good time skiing with his friends.)*

My students persist in literally translating *to have a good time* as **avere un buon tempo.** Never do that!

WARNING

In bocca al lupo!

Perhaps you have an Italian friend facing a difficult situation or a tough exam, and you want to wish them good luck. The literal translation of **buona fortuna!** would work, but this phrase makes you sound really Italian: **In bocca al lupo!** Literally, this means *in the wolf's mouth!* The upcoming difficulty looks like a big wolf, waiting with mouth open wide. Your friend will probably answer **Crepi il lupo!**, which means *May the wolf die!*

Salute!

Someone sneezes and you say **Salute!**, which means health. In fact, it's a way to wish the person to be healthy very soon. *God bless you!* is the English equivalent. You can also use this when making a toast, as in *Cheers!*

Lascia perdere!

Say something is really bugging your new Italian friend. A quick **Lascia perdere!** (*Let it go! Let it be! Forget about it!*) helps put things into a new light. Didn't get the person you courted? Your kid totaled your car but is safe and sound? **Lascia perdere!**

Partita versus Festa

If you want to have a party, you use the word **festa,** and if you're going to a game, you use the word **partita:**

> **I ragazzi hanno una partita di basket dopo scuola oggi.**
> *(The kids have a basketball game after school.)*

> **Mia cugina Kathy dà una festa per Jane e Matthew.**
> *(My cousin Kathy is having a party for Jane and Matthew.)*

Fabbrica versus Stoffa and Fattoria

Even though the word **fabbrica** looks like the word *fabric*, it means *factory*, and the word **fattoria** looks like *factory*, but it means *farm:*

> **La FIAT è una fabbrica italiana di automobili.** *(FIAT is an Italian car factory.)*

> **La stoffa di questo abito è morbido e naturale.** *(This suit's fabric is soft and natural.)*

> **Nella vecchia fattoria ia-ia-o.** *(Old Macdonald had a farm, ee-i-ee-i-o.)*

Appendix

Verb Charts

In this appendix, you can access the conjugations of several tenses of all regular and some irregular Italian verbs, as well as verbs with spelling variations. Use these handy charts as a quick reference to most of your Italian verb needs.

Regular Verbs

The three conjugations of Italian verbs end in **-are**, **-ere**, and **-ire**. Regular verbs follow the same rules for conjugation, no matter the tense (present, past, or future) or mood (imperative, subjunctive, conditional). Note the endings we have in bold.

Regular verbs ending with -are

parlare (to speak, to talk)

Gerund: **parlando**

Past participle: **parlato** *(spoken)* (w/**avere**)

Imperative: parl**a** (**non parlare**), parl**i**, parl**iamo**, parl**ate**, parl**ino**

Present: parl**o**, parl**i**, parl**a**, parl**iamo**, parl**ate**, parl**ano**

Past: **ho parlato**, **hai** parlato, **ha** parlato, **abbiamo** parlato, **avete** parlato, **hanno** parlato

Imperfect: parl**avo**, parl**avi**, parl**ava**, parl**avamo**, parl**avate**, parl**avano**

Future: parler**ò**, parler**ai**, parler**à**, parler**emo**, parler**ete**, parler**anno**

Conditional: parler**ei**, parler**esti**, parler**ebbe**, parler**emmo**, parler**este**, parler**ebbero**

Present Subjunctive: parl**i**, parl**iamo**, parl**iate**, parl**ino**

Other common **-are** verbs include **amare** *(to love)*, **arrivare** *(to arrive)*, **aspettare** *(to wait, to wait for)*, **ballare** *(to dance)*, **cantare** *(to sing)*, **cucinare** *(to cook)*, **disegnare** *(to draw)*, **diventare** *(to become)*, **frequentare** *(to attend, to frequent)*, **giocare** *(to play a game/ sport)*, **imparare** *(to learn)*, **insegnare** *(to teach)*, **lavorare** *(to work)*, **mangiare** *(to eat)*, **pagare** (to pay), **parlare** *(to talk/speak)*, **portare** *(to take, bring)*, **studiare** *(to study)*, **suonare** *(to play an instrument)*, and **tornare** *(to return)*.

Regular verbs ending with -ere

vendere (to sell)

Gerund: vend**endo**

Past participle: vend**uto** *(sold)* (w/**avere**)

Imperative: vend**i**, vend**a**, vend**iamo**, vend**ete**, vend**ano**

Present: vend**o**, vend**i**, vend**e**, vend**iamo**, vend**ete**, vend**ono**

Past: **ho** venduto, **hai** venduto, **ha** venduto, **abbiamo** venduto, **avete** venduto, **hanno** venduto

Imperfect: vend**evo**, vend**evi**, vend**eva**, vend**evamo**, vend**evate**, vend**evano**

Future: vend**erò**, vend**erai**, vend**erà**, vend**eremo**, vend**erete**, vend**eranno**

Conditional: vend**erei**, vend**eresti**, vend**erebbe**, vend**eremmo**, vend**ereste**, vend**erebbero**

Present subjunctive: vend**a**, vend**iamo**, vend**iate**, vend**ano**

Other common **-ere** verbs include **chiedere** *(to ask, to ask for)*, **chiudere** *(to close)*, **dipingere** *(to paint)*, **leggere** *(to read)*, **mettere** *(to put)*, **mordere** *(to bite)*, **perdere** *(to lose)*, **prendere** *(to take, to have)*, **ricevere** *(to receive)*, **ripetere** *(to repeat)*, **scrivere** *(to write)*, **vivere** *(to live)*, **vedere** *(to see)*, **vincere**, *(to win)*, **vivere** *(to live)*. Unlike **vendere** *(to sell)*, most of these **-ere** verbs have irregular past participles: **chiesto, chiuso, dipinto, letto, messo, morso,** perso/perduto, preso, scritto, visto/veduto, vinto, vissuto. *Of this list, only **ricevuto** and **ripetuto** have regular past participles.

Regular verbs ending with -ire*

partire (to leave, depart)

Gerund: **partendo**

Past participle: **partito** *(left)* (w/**essere**)

Imperative: part**i**, part**a**, part**iamo**, part**ite**, part**ano**

Present: part**o**, part**i**, part**e**, part**iamo**, part**ite**, part**ono**

Past: **sono partito/a, sei partito/a, è partito/a, siamo partiti/e, siete partiti/e, sono partiti/e**

Imperfect: part**ivo**, part**ivi**, part**iva**, part**ivamo**, part**ivate**, part**ivano**

Future: partir**ò**, partir**ai**, partir**à**, partir**emo**, partir**ete**, partir**anno**

Conditional: partir**ei**, partir**esti**, partir**ebbe**, partir**emmo**, partir**este**, partir**ebbero**

Present subjunctive: part**a**, part**iamo**, part**iate**, part**ano**

Other common –**ire** verbs include **aprire** *(to open)*, **dormire** *(to sleep)*, **coprire** *(to cover)*, **offrire** *(to offer, to treat)*, and **sentire** *(to hear, feel, taste, touch)*. Note that **aprire** and **coprire** have irregular past participles (**aperto** and **coperto**).

Regular -ire verbs ending with -ire* with -isc- pattern

–**ire** verbs that take the –**isc** only do so in certain persons of the present, imperative, and present subjunctive.

capire (to understand)

Imperative: cap**isci**, cap**isca**, cap**iamo**, cap**ite**, cap**iscano**

Present: cap**isco**, cap**isci**, cap**isce**, cap**iamo**, cap**ite**, cap**iscono**

Present subjunctive: cap**isca**, cap**iscano**

Other common -**isc** verbs include **agire** *(to act)*, **costruire** *(to build)*, **definire** *(to define)*, **finire** *(to finish)*, **interferire** *(to interfere)*, **preferire** *(to prefer)*, **pulire** *(to clean)*, **spedire** *(to send, to mail)*, and **tradire** *(to betray)*.

Spelling-Change Verbs

Some verbs require a spelling change in certain tenses to preserve proper pronunciation.

-care and -gare verbs

For some persons in the present tense, future, conditional, present subjunctive, and imperative (**Lei**, **noi**, **Loro**) you must add an -**h** to keep the hard *k* sound. The additional -**h** is only in the tenses and persons shown below.

cercare (to look for)

Present: cer**ch**i, cer**ch**iamo

Future: cer**ch**erò, cer**ch**erai, cer**ch**erà, cer**ch**eremo, cer**ch**erete, cer**ch**eranno

Conditional: cer**ch**erei, cer**ch**eresti, cer**ch**erebbe, cer**ch**eremmo, cer**ch**ereste, cer**ch**erebbero

Present subjunctive: cer**ch**i, cer**ch**iamo, cer**ch**iate

Imperative: cer**ch**i (Lei), cer**ch**iamo, cer**ch**ino (Loro)

pagare (to pay, to pay for)

Present: pa**gh**i, pa**gh**iamo

Future: pa**gh**erò, pa**gh**erai, pa**gh**erà, pa**gh**eremo, pa**gh**erete, pa**gh**eranno

Conditional: pa**gh**erei, pa**gh**eresti, pa**gh**erebbe, pa**gh**eremmo, pa**gh**ereste, pa**gh**erebbero

Present subjunctive: pa**gh**i, pa**gh**iamo, pa**gh**ino

Imperative: pa**gh**i (Lei), pa**gh**iamo, pa**gh**ino (Loro)

Other verbs ending in -**care** and -**gare** that follow the above schemata include: **dimenticare** *(to forget)*, **giocare** *(to play a sport, cards, board games)*, **leccare** *(to lick)*, **navigare** *(to navigate, to sail)*, **pregare** *(to pray)*, and **traslocare** *(to move/change housing location)*.

-ciare and -giare verbs

For some persons and tenses, verbs ending in -**ciare** and -**giare** undergo a spelling change by dropping the -**i** when creating the future and conditional infinitive stem, to keep the *ch* as in *chart* and *g* sound as in *job*. The -**i** is not pronounced separately from the -**a**, so the sounds are *chah* and *jah*. You also never double up on the -**i**.

mangiare (to eat)

> Present: mang**io**, mang**i**, mang**ia**, mang**iamo**, mang**iate**, mang**iano** (the -**i** isn't repeated)

> Future: mang**erò**, mang**erai**, mang**erà**, mang**eremo**, mang**erete**, mang**eranno**

> Conditional: mang**erei**, mang**eresti**, mang**erebbe**, mang**eremmo**, mang**ereste**, mang**erebbero**

> Present subjunctive: mang**i** (Lei), mang**ino** (Loro)

> Imperative: mang**ia**, mang**i** (Lei), mang**ino** (Loro)

cominciare (to begin)

> Present: comin**cio**, comin**ci**, comin**cia**, comin**ciamo**, comin**ciate** mang**iano** (the -**i** isn't repeated)

> Future: comin**cerò**, comin**cerai**, comin**cerà**, comin**ceremo**, comin**cerete**, comin**ceranno**

> Conditional: comin**cerei**, comin**ceresti**, comin**cerebbe**, comin**ceremmo**, comin**cereste**, comin**cerebbero**

> Present subjunctive: comin**ci** (Lei), comin**cino** (Loro)

> Imperative: comin**cia**, comin**ci** (Lei), comin**cino** (Loro)

Other verbs like **mangiare** ending in -**ciare** and -**giare** include **assaggiare** *(to taste)*, **baciare** *(to kiss)*, **lanciare** *(to launch/throw)*, **passeggiare** *(to stroll)*, and **incoraggiare** *(to encourage)*.

Exception: the verb **studiare** *(to study)*, where the **-i** is pronounced, keeps its **-i** throughout. Another verb like **studiare** is **variare** *(to vary)*.

For example, compare the two future verbs in the following sentence: **Quando studierò a Firenze mangerò la bistecca alla Fiorentina**. *(When I study in Florence I'm going to eat a Florentine-style steak.)*

Reflexive Verbs

lavarsi (to get washed, to wash oneself)

Gerund: **lavando**

Past participle: **lavato** *(washed)* (w/*essere*) *All reflexive verbs take **essere** in a compound past; they also must use reflexive pronouns)

Imperative: lav**a**ti, si lav**i**, lav**iamo**ci, lav**a**tevi, si lav**ino**

Present: mi lav**o**, ti lav**i**, si lav**a**, ci lav**iamo**, vi lav**ate**, si lav**ano**

Past: mi sono lavat**a/o**, ti sei lavat**o/a**, si è lavat**o/a**, ci siamo lavat**i/e**, vi siete lavat**i/e**, ci siamo lavat**i/e**

Imperfect: mi lav**avo**, ti lav**avi**, si lav**ava**, ci lav**avamo**, vi lav**avate**, si lav**avano**

Future: mi laver**ò**, ti laver**ai**, si laver**à**, ci laver**emo**, vi laver**ete**, si laveranno

Conditional: mi laver**ei**, ti laver**esti**, si laver**ebbe**, ci laver**emmo**, vi laver**este**, si laver**ebbero**

Present subjunctive: mi/ti/si lav**i**, ci lav**iamo**, vi lav**iate**, si lav**ino**

Other common reflexive verbs include: **addormentarsi** *(to fall asleep)*, **alzarsi** *(to get up)*, **arrabbiarsi** *(to get angry)*, **divertirsi** *(to have fun)*, **farsi la barba** *(to shave)*, **innamorarsi** *(to fall in love)*, **mettersi** *(to put [something] on)*, **permettersi** *(to afford)*, **sentirsi** *(to feel)*, **sposarsi** *(to get married)*, **svegliarsi** *(to wake up)*, and **vestirsi** *(to get dressed)*.

Irregular Verbs

Irregular verbs may undergo changes in some or all tenses and moods, and for some or all subjects. Memorize the irregular forms (bolded here) because they follow no specific rules; memorize the bolded endings as well.

avere (to have)

Gerund: **avendo**

Past Participle: **avuto** *(had)* (w/**avere**)

Imperative: **abbi, abbia, abbiamo, abbiate, abbiano**

Present: **ho, hai, ha, abbiamo,** av**ete, hanno**

Past: **ho avuto, hai** avuto, **ha** avuto, **abbiamo** avuto, **avete** avuto, **hanno** avuto

Imperfect: av**evo,** av**evi,** av**eva,** av**evamo,** av**evate,** av**evano**

Future: avr**ò,** avr**ai,** avr**à,** avr**emo,** avr**ete,** avr**anno**

Conditional: avr**ei,** avr**esti,** avr**ebbe,** avr**emmo,** avr**este,** avr**ebbero**

Present subjunctive: **abbia, abbiamo, abbiate, abbiano**

essere (to be)

Gerund: **essendo**

Past Participle: **stato** *(been)* (w/*essere*)

Imperative: **sii, sia, siamo, siate, siano**

Present: **sono, sei, è, siamo, siete, sono**

Past: **sono stato/a, sei** stato/a, è stato/a, **siamo** stat**i/e, siete** stat**i/e, sono** stat**i/e**

Imperfect: **ero, eri, era, eravamo, eravate, erano**

Future: **sarò, sarai, sarà, saremo, sarete, saranno**

Conditional: **sarei, saresti, sarebbe, saremmo, sareste, sarebbero**

Present subjunctive: **sia, siamo, siate, siano**

andare (to go)

Gerund: **andando**

Past participle: **andato** *(went, gone)* (w/**essere**)

Imperative: **vai/va', vada, vadano**

Present: **vado, vai, va**, and**iamo**, and**ate, vanno**

Past: sono andat**o/a**, sei andat**o/a**, è andat**o/a**, siamo andat**i/e**, siete andat**i/e**, sono andat**i/e**

Future: **andrò, andrai, andrà, andremo, andrete, andranno**

Conditional: **andrei, andresti, andrebbe, andremmo, andreste, andrebbero**

Present subjunctive: **vada, andiate, vadano**

bere (to drink)

Gerund: **bevendo**

Past participle: **bevuto** *(drank, drunk)* (w/**avere**)

Imperative: bev**i**, bev**a**, bev**iamo**, bev**ete**, bev**ano**

Present: bev**o**, bev**i**, bev**e**, bev**iamo**, bev**ete**, bev**ono**

Past: **ho bevuto, hai bevuto, ha bevuto, abbiamo bevuto, avete bevuto, hanno bevuto**

Imperfect: bev**evo**, bev**evi**, bev**eva**, bev**evamo**, bev**evate**, bev**evano**

Future: **berrò, berrai, berrà, berremo, berrete, berranno**

Conditional: **berrei, berresti, berrebbe, berremmo, berreste, berrebbero**

Present subjunctive: bev**a**, bev**iamo**, bev**iate**, bev**ano**

dare (to give)

Gerund: **parlando**

Past participle: **dato** *(gave, given)* (w/**avere**)

Imperative: **dai/da', dia, diamo, date, diano**

Present: d**o**, d**ai** d**à**, d**iamo**, d**ate**, d**anno**

Future: **darò, darai, darà, daremo, darete, daranno**

Conditional: **darei, daresti, darebbe, daremmo, dareste, darebbero**

Present subjunctive: **dia,** d**iamo,** d**iate, diano**

dire (to say)

Gerund: **dicendo**

Past participle: **detto** *(said)* (w/**avere**)

Imperative: **di', dica, diciamo, dite, dicano**

Present: **dico, dici, dice, diciamo, dite, dicono**

Imperfect: **dicevo, dicevi, diceva, dicevamo, dicevate, dicevano**

Present subjunctive: **dica, diciate, dicano**

dovere: (ought to, should, must)

Gerund: **dovendo**

Past participle: **dovuto** *(had to, needed to)* (w/**avere**)

Present: **devo, devi, deve, dobbiamo,** dovete, **devono**

Future: **dovrò, dovrai, dovrà, dovremo, dovrete, dovranno**

Conditional: **dovrei, dovresti, dovrebbe, dovremmo, dovreste, dovrebbero**

Present subjunctive: **debba, dobbiamo, dobbiate, debbano**

fare (to do or make)

Gerund: **facendo**

Past participle: **fatto** *(done, made)* (w/**avere**)

Imperative: **fai/fa', faccia, facciamo, fate, facciano**

Present: **faccio, fai, fa, facciamo, fate, fanno**

Past: ho **fatto,** hai **fatto,** ha **fatto,** abbiamo **fatto,** avete **fatto,** hanno **fatto**

Imperfect: **facevo, facevi, faceva, facevamo, facevate, facevano**

Future: **farò, farai, farà, faremo, farete, faranno**

Conditional: **farei, faresti, farebbe, faremmo, fareste, farebbero**

Present subjunctive: **faccia, facciamo, facciate, facciano**

morire (to die)

Gerund: **morendo**

Past participle: **morto** *(died)* (w/**essere**)

Imperative: **muori, muoia, moriamo, morite, muoiano**

Present: **muoio, muori, muore,** moriamo, morite, **muoiono**

Past: **sono morto/a,** sei **morto/a,** è **morto/a,** siamo **morti/e,** siete **morti/e,** sono **morti/e**

Present subjunctive: **muoia, moriate, muoiano**

piacere (to like)

The verb **piacere** takes indirect object pronouns and you usually only need the third person singular and plural of this verb. *mi/ti/gli/le/ci/vi/gli (loro)*

Gerund: **piacendo**

Past participle: **piaciuto** *(liked)* (w/**essere**)

Present: **piace, piacciono**

Past: **è piaciuto/a, sono piaciuti/e**

Imperfect: **piaceva, piacevano**

Future: **piacerà, piaceranno**

Conditional: **piacerebbe, piacerebbero**

Present subjunctive: **piaccia, piacciano**

potere (to be able to, may, can)

Gerund: **potendo**

Past participle: **potuto** *(could)* (w/**avere**, usually)

Present: **posso, puoi, può, possiamo, possono**

Future: **potrò, potrai, potrà, potremo, potrete, potranno**

Conditional: **potrei, potresti, potrebbe, potremmo, potreste, potrebbero**

Present subjunctive: **possa, possiamo, possiate, possano**

rimanere (to stay, to remain)

Gerund: **rimanendo**

Past participle: **rimasto** *(stayed, remained)* (w/**essere**)

Imperative: **rimanga, rimangano**

Present: **rimango**, rimani, rimane, riman**iamo**, riman**ete, rimangono**

Past: sono **rimasto/a**, sei **rimasto/a**, è **rimasto/a**, siamo **rimasti/e**, siete **rimasti/e**, sono **rimasti/e**

Future: **rimarrò, rimarrai, rimarrà, rimarremo, rimarrete, rimarranno**

Conditional: **rimarrei, rimarresti, rimarrebbe, rimarremmo, rimarreste, rimarrebbero**

Present subjunctive: **rimanga, rimaniate, rimangano**

salire (to ascend, go up, board-get in/on [a plane, boat, car, train])

Gerund: **salendo**

Past participle: **salito** *(ascended, went up)* (w/**essere**)

Imperative: sal**ga**, sal**gano**

Present: sal**go,** sal**gono**

Present subjunctive: sal**ga**, sal**gano**

sapere (to know)

Gerund: **sapendo**

Past participle: **saputo** *(knew, have known)* (w/**avere**)

Imperative: **sappi, sappia, sappiate, sappiamo, sappiano**

Present: **so, sai, sa, sappiamo,** sap**ete, sanno**

Future: **saprò, saprai, saprà, sapremo, saprete, sapranno**

Conditional: **saprei, sapresti, saprebbe, sapremmo, sapreste, saprebbero**

Present subjunctive: **sappia, sappiate, sappiamo, sappiano**

scegliere (to choose)

Gerund: **scegliendo**

Past participle: **scelto** *(chose, chosen)* (w/**avere**)

Imperative: **scelga, scelgano**

Present: **scelgo, scegli, sceglie, scegliamo, scegliete, scelgono**

Past: **ho scelto**

Present subjunctive: **scelga, scegliate, scelgano**

sedersi (to sit)

Gerund: **sedendo**

Past participle: **seduto** *(sat)* (w/**essere**)

Imperative: **siedi**ti, si **sieda**, si **siedano**

Present: mi **siedo**, ti **siedi**, si **siede**, ci sed**iamo**, vi sed**ete**, si **siedono**

Past: mi sono sed**uto/a**

Future: mi **siederò**, ti **siederai**, si **siederà**, ci **siederemo**, vi **siederete**, si **siederanno**

Conditional: mi **siederei**, ti **siederesti**, si **siederebbe**, ci **siederemmo**, vi **siedereste**, si **siederebbero**

Present subjunctive: mi/ti/si **sieda**, ci sed**iamo**, vi **sediate**, si **siedano**

stare (to stay, to be)

Gerund: **stando**

Past participle: **stato** *(stayed, was)* (w/**essere**)

Imperative: **sta/sta'**, st**ia**, st**iamo**, st**ate**, st**iano**

Present: st**o**, sta**i**, st**a**, st**iamo**, st**ate**, st**anno**

Past: sono stat**o/a**

Future: **starò, starai, starà, staremo, starete, staranno**

Conditional: **starei, staresti, starebbe, staremmo, stareste, starebbero**

Present subjunctive: **stia, stiate, stiano**

tradurre (to translate)

Gerund: **traducendo**

Past participle: **tradotto** *(translated)* (w/**avere**)

Imperative: trad**uci**, trad**uca**, trad**uciamo**, trad**ucete**, trad**ucano**

Present: trad**uco**, trad**uci**, trad**uce**, trad**uciamo**, trad**ucete**, trad**ucono**

Past: **ho tradotto**

Present subjunctive: trad**uca**, trad**uciamo**, trad**uciate**, trad**ucano**

Other verbs that follow the structure of **tradurre** include **dedurre** (*to deduce*) and **produrre** (*to produce*).

uscire (to go out)

Gerund: **uscendo**

Past participle: **uscito** *(went out)* (w/**essere**)

Imperative: **esci, esca,** usc**iamo**, usc**ite**, **escano**

Present: **esco, esci, esce,** usc**iamo**, usc**ite**, **escono**

Past: sono usc**ito/a**

Present subjunctive: **esca,** usc**iamo**, usc**iate**, **escano**

venire (to come)

Gerund: **venendo**

Past participle: **venuto** *(came)* (w/**essere**)

Imperative: **venga, vengano**

Present: **vengo, vieni, viene,** veniamo, ven**i**te, **vengono**

Past: sono ven**uto/a**

Present subjunctive: **venga, veniate, vengano**

volere (to want)

Gerund: **volendo**

Past participle: **voluto** *(sold)* (w/**avere,** usually)

Present: **voglio, vuoi, vuole, vogliamo,** vol**e**te, **vogliono**

Past: ho vol**uto**

Future: **vorrò, vorrai, vorrà, vorremo, vorrete, vorranno**

Conditional: **vorrei, vorresti, vorrebbe, vorremmo, vorreste, vorrebbero**

Present subjunctive: **voglia, vogliamo, vogliate, vogliano**

Index

F

fabbrica (factory), 164

family, using possessive adjectives with, 39–40

fare (to do/to make), 138, 146, 173–174

fare domanda (to apply), 161–162

fare il bagno (to take a bath/to go for a swim), 162

fare una domanda (to ask a question), 161–162

fattoria (farm), 164

feminine nouns, 27–29

festa, 164

formal greetings/salutations, 10–12

funzionare (to work), 162

future tense, 23–24, 131–132

  common expressions, 133

  futuro anteriore (future perfect), 140–141

  futuro semplice (simple future tense), 134–140

  prediction with (futuro di probabilità), 141–142

  using, 132–133

  using present to talk about future, 134

futuro anteriore (future perfect), 140–141

futuro semplice (simple future tense), 134–140

G

g (consonant), pronunciation of, 8

-gare verbs, 151, 168–169

gender, 25–26

  gendered words, 24

of nouns, 24–31

and object pronouns, 41–43

and possessive adjectives, 36–40

gerunds, 70–71

-giare verbs, 151, 169–170

giocare (to play a sport, cards), 52, 162

gl, pronunciation of, 9

gn, pronunciation of, 9

greetings, 10–13

H

h (consonant), pronunciation of, 9

I

i (vowel), 7

idiomatic expressions, 64

imperative mood, 143–149

  adding pronouns to commands, 147–148

  formal imperatives of regular verbs, 145–146

  informal imperatives of regular verbs, 144–145

  irregular verbs, 146–147

  negative commands, 147

  reflexives, 148–149

imperfetto, 109, 123–129

  irregular verbs in, 124–126

  key terms associated with, 128–129

  recognizing regular verbs in, 123–124

  sapere and conoscere in, 129

  uses of, 126–127

impersonal expressions, 154–155

in (in/into/to/by), 92–94, 96

In bocca al lupo!, 163

indefinite articles, 22, 32, 35–36

indicative mood, 143, 144

indirect object pronouns, 42–43

infinitives, 46, 51–56

informal greetings/salutations, 12–13

innamorarsi (to fall in love), 69

interrogatives, 61, 99–105. *See also* questions

intransitive verbs, 115–120

invariable adjectives, 75, 78

invariable nouns, 30–31

-ire verbs, 51, 54–56, 61–62, 70–71, 124, 167–168

-ire/isc verbs, 54–56, 71, 167–168

irregular adjectives, 78

irregular comparatives/superlatives, 88–90

irregular past participles, 112–114

irregular verbs, 23, 57–64, 71, 171–178

  in futuro semplice, 137–140

  imperatives of, 146–147

  in imperfetto, 124–126

  in present conditional tense, 158–159

  present subjunctive, 152–154

  stem-changing, 139–140

L

Lascia perdere! (Let it go! Let it be! Forget about it!), 164

R

reflexive pronouns, 66, 148
reflexive verbs, 40, 66–69, 170
  forming, 66–69
  imperatives, 149
  piacere (to like/to be pleasing to), 69
  usage of, 65–66
regular adjectives, 74–77
regular past participles, 111–112
regular verbs, 23, 51–56, 165–168
  in futuro semplice, 134–137
  imperatives of, 144–146
  in imperfetto, 123–124
  in present conditional tense, 157–159
  stem-changing, 136–137
relative superlatives, 87–89
rimanere (to stay/to remain), 175

S

salire (to ascend/go up/board-get in/on [a plane, boat, car, train]), 175
salutations, 12–13
Salute!, 163
sapere (to know), 60–61, 129, 159, 175–176
scegliere (to choose), 176
sedersi (to sit), 176
sempre meno, 86
sempre più, 86
simple prepositions (preposizioni semplici), 90–91
simple sentences, 24
simple tenses, 23–24
stare (to be/to stay), 138–139, 146, 176–177
stoffa (fabric), 164
stress, 9–10
studiare (to study), 136
su (on/onto), 95
subject pronouns, 23, 47–50
  formal use of, 49–50
  and inclusion, 47–48
  informal use of, 48–50
  usage of, 48
subjunctive mood, 143, 149–156
  impersonal expressions, 154–155
  irregular present subjunctive verbs, 152–153
  past subjunctive, 155–156
  present subjunctive, 150–153
  verbs and expressions requiring, 153–154
suonare (to play an instrument), 53, 162
superlatives, 83, 87–90

T

time, 19–21, 122
tradurre (to translate), 126, 177
transitive verbs, 115–116

U

u (vowel), 7
uscire (to go out), 62, 177

V

vendere (to sell), 124, 166
venire (to come), 61, 177–178
verbs, 23, 46. See also mood
  irregular, 23, 57–64, 71, 124–126, 137–140, 146–147, 158–159, 171–178
  modal, 59–60
  reflexive, 40, 66–69, 148, 170
  regular, 23, 51–56, 123–124, 134–137, 144–146, 157–158, 165–168
  spelling-change, 168–170
volere (to want), 60, c158, 178
vowels, 7

About the Author

Teresa L. Picarazzi, PhD, has been teaching Italian for 40 years. Teresa has taught at Dartmouth College, the University of Arizona, Wesleyan University, and Fairfield University. Teresa also recently retired, after 20 years, from teaching at the Hopkins School (New Haven, CT.). She was the 2021 recipient of the AATI Distinguished Service Award, K-12 (American Association of Teachers of Italian). Teresa has lived, studied, and worked in Cortona, Ferrara, Urbino, Siena, Florence, and Ravenna. Teresa loves to spend the summer in Ravenna with her husband Giancarlo, and daughter Emilia.

Dedication

This book wouldn't exist, and I wouldn't know how to teach, without my students, and so I dedicate it — again — with love to all of my students, present and past.

Author's Acknowledgments

I have to thank several people for helping me complete this book. First, Acquisitions Editor Lindsay Berg at Wiley for bringing me on to work on another project — my fifth project! — for *For Dummies*, Project Editor and Copy Editor Chad Sievers, for his careful reading and thoughtful queries, and for helping me keep deadlines, and Technical Editor Bijou D'Arpa for her attentive reading and crucial comments. (Any errors you find in this book are entirely my responsibility.) A huge thanks goes to my agent, Marilyn Allen, for her grace and patience. Thank you as well to my parents, Mary and Domenico Picarazzi, for instilling in me their inspiring work ethic and for actively cheering me on, always. Finally, I need to thank Giancarlo and Emilia for putting up with me and for encouraging me to take on this project.

Publisher's Acknowledgments

Acquisition Editors: Lindsay Berg and Shannon Kucaj

Project Manager and Copy Editor: Chad R. Sievers

Senior Managing Editor: Kristie Pyles

Technical Editor: Beatrice "Bijou" D'Arpa

Production Editor: Bharaneedharan Murthy

Cover Design and Image: Wiley